THE VERSE
BY THE
SIDE
OF THE
ROAD:

The Story of the Burma-Shave Signs and Jingles

Frank Rowsome, Jr.

Drawings by CARL ROSE

A PLUME BOOK

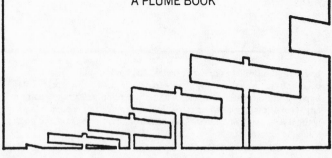

PLUME
Published by the Penguin Group
Penguin Books USA Inc., 375 Hudson Street, New York, New York
10014, U.S.A.
Penguin Books Ltd, 27 Wrights Lane, London W8 5TZ, England
Penguin Books Australia Ltd, Ringwood, Victoria, Australia
Penguin Books Canada Ltd, 10 Alcorn Avenue, Toronto, Ontario,
Canada M4V 3B2
Penguin Books (N.Z.) Ltd, 182-190 Wairau Road, Auckland 10,
New Zealand

Penguin Books Ltd, Registered Offices: Harmondsworth, Middlesex,
England

Published by Plume, an imprint of New American Library,
a division of Penguin Books USA Inc.

First published in 1965 by The Stephen Greene Press

10 9 8 7 6 5 4 3 2

 REGISTERED TRADEMARK—MARCA REGISTRADA

Printed in the United States of America

Contents

Foreword

The signs now roll by in the mind, gone but not forgotten. Few images bring back the good old days faster than a speeding Burma-Shave sign. Of course, the signs weren't speeding, it just seemed that way.

No doubt about it, the hypnotic attraction of the "verse by the side of the road" was irresistible. Once that first Burma-Shave sign came into view you were hooked, all the way to the tantalizing punch line. Did anyone, anywhere, fail to twist their necks to read them? Or not hurry a guess as to what the final sign might say?

It's the kind of Americana you just don't see anymore. Oh, you can still spot a few signs hyping the approach of some reptile farm, or super duper drug store, but it isn't the same. You can't beat the simple beauty — the genius — of those Burma-Shave classics.

It all started in 1927, during the early years of America's romance with the automobile and the open road. It had quite a run, too; all the way to 1963 when the powerful lure of television and radio advertising finally forced Burma-Shave off the road.

Growing up on the high plains of Kansas during the dust bowl years, I still remember the signs. They were as much a part of the scenery as the wheatfields and cattle.

The big cities may have had outdoor ads the size of a ten story building, or cigarette billboards that blew smoke rings, but rural America had Burma-Shave. We had the space, the ruler-straight roads the staggered signs needed and, judging by the Burma-Shave message, the heaviest beards in America.

This book will take you back to a simpler, more innocent era, when a two-lane road was a super highway, and a car trip from Russell, Kansas to Kansas City was like going all the way to Paris.

I am honored to write the introduction for this special 25th anniversary edition of *The Verse by the Side of the Road*. It is an all-American success story.

Let me tell you, we have all been touched by the Burma-Shave brush:

> In politics
> It's always safer
> Not to make waves
> It's not my style
> I've had some close shaves

— *Bob Dole*

1:

Remember, Remember

LIKE SO MUCH ELSE, the cars too were different in those days. The last of the spidery but agile Model T Fords had scurried off the production line in May 1927, having been overtaken in the national preference by the disk-wheeled Chevy. Its replacement, the Model A Ford—a nifty vehicle equipped with such elegances as windshield wings, four-wheel brakes, and an authentic gearshift lever sprouting from the floor—was now offered in colors other than black. It was unveiled nationally, in a masterly flurry of exploitation, on December 2, 1927, when thousands queued patiently outside showrooms for their first glimpse of the new wonder.

There were, in those springtime days of America's love affair with its automobiles, many other beloveds. There was the doughty Dodge, as reliable as an Airedale despite its willfully mixed-up gearshift pattern; the substantial Reo and Buick; the sprightly Pontiac and Overland; the Willys- and Stearns-Knights with their exotic sleeve valves; and the radical, warily regarded, air-cooled Franklin. For owners who disdained the commonplace there were ponderous Lincolns and Cadillacs; long-hooded Packards, special favorites with prospering bootleggers; and the lordly, spacious Pierce-Arrow, its wide-apart headlights staring with hauteur. For sportier tastes there were Kissels and Jordans, Auburns and Dusenbergs, Marmons and Templars, as well as the celebrated Stutz, a potent chariot that Cannonball Baker drove from city to city (making his runs in the after-midnight hours when traffic was lightest) at awesome averages of 55 and even 60 mph.

This was not, of course, the way most of us drove. Instead we climbed up—a two-stage ascent—into Old Betsy (very possibly a Studebaker or Nash, an Essex or Peerless) and set forth on our family Sunday-afternoon drive. We were perhaps headed for Nantasket Beach, or all the way around the lake, or out beyond Fort Loudon to

Mr. Welch's roadside stand where, among the brightly painted windmills, there would be an opportunity to buy some freshly picked corn or cucumbers. Because this trip might, with variation and caprice, amount to as much as sixty or sixty-five miles, we prudently stopped at Snow's Garage down on Village Avenue for gasoline, oil, and, if need be, free air and water.

Snow's had by now largely outworn its livery-stable origin. The red gasoline pump stood near the door, topped by a glass cylinder into which the fuel was pumped, thence to descend by gravity into the tank between the half-elliptic springs by Betsy's spare tire. Snow's also had a portable gasoline pump, a wheeled rectangular cart with a cranked pump, and this could be trundled out in the event that two cars needed fuel at the same time. If Betsy should need some oil, it was dispensed from a barrel into a quart measure and funneled into her engine. (Snow's newest and most formidable competitor, an oil-company gas station across the street, had already begun to serve up its beautiful dark-green oil in prefilled glass bottles, each with a screwed-on spout and carried out in a compartmented wire basket, like milk bottles.)

At the end of town, just before the sharp turn and the striped wooden barriers that guarded the railroad crossing, there was a red-and-green traffic light hung out over the intersection. Everyone in town was very pleased with that traffic light. Not for us the primitive pipe-and-painted-tin semaphores, dutifully swiveled by the policeman on duty. The red-and-green light symbolized the town's growth and importance, and the increasing flow of traffic coming through on State Route 31. We admitted, to be sure, that State 31 really wasn't at all like the celebrated Lincoln Highway, an awesome transcontinental artery, two lanes wide and with red-white-and-blue markers painted on its adjoining telegraph poles. It was said that along the Lincoln Highway you could often glimpse dusty,

THE TWENTIES~

FEMALE
HIGH FASHION

FEMALE
POUR LE SPORT

GAS

GAS

GASOLINE PUMP

OVERNIGHT
CABIN

ENTRANCE TO
A TAVERN

SPEED 25
MILES PER HOUR

PROFILE OF A TWO LANE STATE HIGHWAY

A PARTIAL PANORAMA

POPULAR
BALLROOM
DANCE

DEALER
IN WINE
& SPIRITS

MALE
COUNTRY
CLUB ATTIRE

MALE
WINTER
PLUMAGE

A PRESIDENT OF
THE UNITED STATES

INCLUDING POPULAR CARS OF THE TIME

powerful cars with extra containers of fuel, oil, and water affixed to their running boards, and even with rope and axes for possible use during difficult passages coast to coast.

The highways, as well as the cars, were different and changing in the Twenties. Once out of town they still narrowed down to two lanes, narrow enough so that you warily surveyed each oncoming car for any tendencies toward road-hogging. Even when a two-lane road wasn't awkwardly narrow, drivers had to practice a routine now in relative disuse: the complex art of overtaking and passing another car. This was tricky, calling for skill, patience, resolution, and a knowledge of just how briskly Betsy could get out and around. Sometimes a driver misjudged and had to break off and tuck in behind, his face darkening with embarrassment and anger.

Curves there were in abundance in those days. Some rose naturally from the pre-automobile perambulations of roads. Even in the section-line Midwestern states, where curves were far less common, a sudden T-shaped corner (perhaps originating from property lines) could bring to a somnolent driver the humiliation of having to back out of an alfalfa field. Some curves were purely man made, arising from the parsimonious calculations of highway departments which held that the shortest bridge was the cheapest, even if it did mean a turn at each end. And curves occurred abundantly in the vertical plane as well, for this was long before earthmovers had developed their prodigious ability to cut and fill. Many small tads, perched back in the tonneau of the family touring car, would beseech a parent to drive *faster, faster* on the "roller-coaster road," sometimes called shoot-the-chutes or bump-the-bumps.

Often a picnic lunch was taken, with the food packed in advance, according to the custom of the Twenties, rather than, as now, with oddments flung into an alu-

6

minum ice chest. There were hard-boiled eggs (with a pinch of salt folded in a square of waxed paper); a shoebox of sandwiches, perhaps peanut butter and jam, or slices of corned beef, or ham and cheese. There'd also be soda crackers, a tin of deviled ham (with wonderful forked-tail red imps on the wrapper), and a jar of stuffed olives. There'd be a bag of potato chips, some cold roast chicken that had been located at the extreme back of the icebox, a supply of grapes or oranges and tangerines, cold milk in the Thermos, and bottles of ginger ale or grape juice for those grown up, or almost so. All this would be neatly stowed in a wicker hamper. When opened by the side of the road thirty miles from home, the hamper would be found to lack an opener for the deviled ham or the bottles. This lack would, among cries of recrimination, be ultimately remedied by use of the pliers and screwdriver from Betsy's toolbox, at the cost of no more than a spilled and fuzzing mouthful of ginger ale, and an injured expression on the face of the mother or aunt who had packed the lunch.

Those years of the Twenties were ones of continuous change. The roads grew steadily better, as did the cars. It was no longer necessary to carry elaborate kits for roadside tire repairs. And where the old car had had a natural cruising speed of about 35 mph and became excited at speeds above 45, displaying a disquieting tendency to lunge, the new Model A Fords or Chevys or Overlands were perfectly willing to lope all day long at 50, and had the brakes to suit. As the driving radius extended, it was no longer feasible to brag about a 225-mile day. More and more we took highway vacation trips. Roadside cabins began to appear—one- or two-room dollhouses arranged in an arc, with whitewashed stones outlining the curve of the driveway. They could be rented for two dollars or three dollars a night and were noticeably more convenient than tourist rooms, as well as cheaper

7

than the Hotel Majestic downtown, where it was necessary to put on a necktie to confront the room clerk. Social historians should record the effect of cabins on, among other things, sports clothes, the practice of traveling with pets, and the growth of an additional meaning for the word "vacancy."

In times of continuous change it is difficult to recognize small beginnings. But in the fall of 1925, and again during the following year, one small beginning took place that would later catch the fancy of, and amuse, whole generations of highway-faring Americans.

2:

On the Road
to Red Wing

"My GRANDFATHER was an attorney in the early days of Minneapolis. In those times lawyers were short on education and long on enterprise, and Grandfather had each of these attributes. For a time he was the U.S. marshal here, with the duty of apprehending men who sold liquor to the Indians. In his law office he also manufactured a liniment—lawyers were into all kinds of things then, because in those days law practice wasn't as fruitful as it is now."

The speaker was Leonard Odell, a husky, broad-shouldered man in his late fifties, the president of the Burma-Vita Company, a division of Philip Morris, Inc. Odell was recounting the early beginnings of Burma-Shave to a recent visitor to the firm's plant on the western outskirts of Minneapolis. Beyond the executive-office walls, mixing and packaging machinery occasionally made staccato and profitable noises. Outside the window and beyond the freight siding Bassett's Creek and a city park could be glimpsed.

"He claimed he'd procured the liniment recipe from an old sea captain, and perhaps he did. Of course most all of those liniments came from sea captains; they traveled the world and encountered witch doctors and collected secret potions. Anyhow, Grandfather made it in his office up in the old Globe Building. It was a potent liniment both in action and smell. You could smell it on the ground floor when he was mixing it on the fifth floor, which probably didn't endear him to his fellow tenants. But he made it there for many years, selling it through a couple of drugstores in lower Minneapolis.

"His son, Clinton, was educated in law at the University of Minnesota, and he was a practicing attorney. Dad was also in the insurance business, and he was a very successful man. He founded the White-Odell agency, which, at one time, had more insurance on its books than

10

any other single agency in the United States. Dad was a *whale* of a salesman. He worked hard, probably too hard, because in 1920 he took sick—sciatic rheumatism, nerve disorders, couldn't walk. He was miserable. Took him pretty near three years to get the thing cured so he could walk again. He climbed out of his illness about 1923, when I was in high school and my brother Allan was at the University. The doctors told him he shouldn't try anything hard-driving again if he wanted to keep his health.

"Well, the family all had this liniment in their homes. I had an aunt who was burned severely on the hand about then with hot fat. In desperation she stuck her hand into this liniment, and in spite of what you might think, the pain stopped immediately. She had no blisters and no scars. It was a marvelous thing.

"So Dad, casting around for something to do, said maybe we can market this. My grandfather had had a stroke by then, and was confined to the house, and Dad was taking care of him. Dad made a royalty arrangement with him and we set out to sell it. We called it Burma-Vita. *Burma* because most of the essential oils in the liniment came from the Malay peninsula and Burma, and *Vita* from the Latin for life and vigor—the whole name meaning Life from Burma.

"Well, we sure starved to death on that product for a couple of years. With a liniment you have to catch a customer who isn't feeling well, and even when you do you only sell him once in a while. The wholesale drug company in town, the people that we got the ingredients from, kept reminding Dad that it would be better if we could find something we could sell everybody, all the time, instead of just hunting for people who were sick. They gave Dad some Lloyd's Euxesis to see what he thought of it.

"Now Lloyd's Euxesis, made in England, was the original brushless shaving cream on the world market. It was a sticky, gummy substance. Still, as an old traveling man, Dad could see the advantage of a brushless shaving cream. You didn't have to pack that wet brush in your grip, where it would mildew and get foul-smelling before you got home. (Remember how they used to get green at the base?)

"Some time before, Dad had heard about a chemist in town who had taken seriously sick, perhaps fatally, and had pulled up stakes for Arizona to see if he could recover. Dad was touched by the story, and in December he wrote him a note with a check for twenty-five dollars, and wished him a merry Christmas. Well, it was about a year later, in 1925, when we were close to the low ebb of all time with the liniment, when the door opened and in walked this chemist, Carl Noren. He said 'Here I am, and I'm well, and what can I do for you?'

"Dad said 'What do you know about a brushless shaving cream?' Carl said 'I never heard of one.' Dad tossed him a tube of Lloyd's Euxesis and said 'Can you make a better one than this?' Carl took a look at it and said 'Well, I can sure try—I used to be chief cosmetic chemist for the old Minneapolis Drug Company.' Then Carl picked up the phone and ordered the ingredients that he thought he'd need, and about three o'clock that afternoon batch number one of Burma-Shave came off the fire. It was, frankly, terrible stuff. We had formulations on and off the market about three times. It wasn't until we got to Formula One Forty-three that we came up with a good, stable product. Actually we'd gone by it and were up close to Formula Three Hundred, and then Dad discovered some of old One Forty-three left in a jar and got a real fine shave from it. That's how we discovered that, if you *aged* old One Forty-three for two or three months, you got a fine shave with it.

"All of us went out and tried to market it. My brother Allan was down in Joliet, Illinois, working with a program that we called Jars on Approval. You'd just walk into a man's office and say 'Here's a jar of Burma-Shave.' 'What's *that*?' he'd ask. You'd explain and tell him how to use it. You'd say 'Take it home and try it and if you like it, give me fifty cents when I come back next week. If you don't, just give me back what's left then and we'll still be friends.'

"Jars on Approval—if you want to starve to death fast, that's one way to do it. I guess Al was pretty discouraged. One day on the road between Aurora and Joliet he saw a set of small serial signs advertising a gas station: Gas, Oil, Restrooms, things like that—maybe a dozen of them—and then at the end a sign would point in to the gas station. Al thought 'Every time I see one of these setups, I read every one of the signs. So why can't you sell a product that way?'

"Well, it sounded good to me, and to everyone else. Except when he came home to tell Dad about his idea, Dad said 'The trouble with you is that you're homesick.' But Dad talked to some of the big advertising men here, and in Chicago—and they said that, year in and year out, it would never work. But Allan sold Dad on giving him two hundred dollars to try out his idea. I think Dad did it more to shut him up than anything else.

"We bought secondhand boards over at the Rose Brothers Wrecking Company. They had plenty of nail-holes in them and some were burned on one side. We sawed them up into thirty-six-inch lengths and painted them up, using a thin brass stencil and brush. They were pretty crude. These signs didn't have rhymes or jingles— just what you might call prose: SHAVE THE MODERN WAY / FINE FOR THE SKIN / DRUGGISTS HAVE IT / BURMA-SHAVE. It was getting on into the fall of 1925, and we had to hurry like the dickens to get them into the ground before it froze solid. We put them on two roads out of Minneapolis. One was Route Sixty-five to Albert Lea, and the other was the road to Red Wing. Maybe we had ten or twelve sets of signs on those two highways.

"By the start of the year we were getting the first re-peat orders we'd ever had in the history of the company— all from druggists serving people who traveled those roads. As he watched those repeat orders rolling in, Dad began to feel that maybe the boys were thinking all right, after all. He called us in and said 'Allan, I believe you've got a real great idea here. It's tremendous. The only trouble is, we're broke.'

"With this, Dad did one of the greatest sales jobs I've ever heard of. He had a busted company, he had a

14

product that most people had never heard of, much less believed in, and he had an advertising idea that ad men said wouldn't work. With these three things going for him, he incorporated and then went out and sold forty-nine percent of the stock in less than three weeks. This testified not only to his sales ability but also to the fact that he was a highly respected man that a lot of people had confidence in.

"So early in 1926 we set up our first sign shop. Using slogans and selling lines that Dad and Al thought up, we made a pile of silk-screen signs that weren't *quite* as crude as those first stenciled ones. And Al went out ahead and bought the locations, and I came along behind and dug the holes and tamped in the posts. Boy, did I learn this business starting from three feet under ground."

Leonard Odell walked over to the window, looking out over Bassett's Creek to the parkland beyond. "If you watch for a moment, you can almost always see a pheasant," he told his visitor. "There are thousands of them now. You know, Dad helped import the first pheasants into this state. He was a great conservationist. Made a hobby out of wildflowers, too. He was active in civic affairs and good politics. A hard-driving and conscientious man, with a lot of friends. After that spring we were on our way, and we had a lot of fun over the years. Boy, was Dad enthusiastic! He was a real stem-winder."

3:

And Oh Louise

THE ESSENTIAL SPIRIT of Burma-Shave—what made America first notice and later cherish the jaunty little signs—was of course their light-heartedness. Humor has always been infrequent in advertising, and in the years of the Depression it was so scarce as to be virtually a trace element. If one examines the newspapers and magazines of the period the nearest in the way of intentional humor one is likely to find is an occasional spasm of jocosity, as when an artist would depict a chubby, golden-ringleted female toddler, so busy holding her ice-cream cone above the leaps of a frisky puppy that her defective suspenders threaten to disclose her infant buttocks.

They were days when many advertisers preferred long blocks of copy, composed around the "reason why" principle. In drugstore products in particular, with business poor and competition fierce, many advertisers were aiming single-mindedly for the jugular. Listerine and Lifebuoy were instilling the thought that each citizen was needlessly malodorous; Absorbine Jr. was developing the concept that many apparently beautiful women had cracked and scabby toes; and numerous national advertisers, from Fleischmann's Yeast to Feenamint, were preaching the doctrine that infrequent and faulty bowel movements were both a national disgrace and a grievous personal failure.

It was upon this advertising scene—a lapel-grabbing, intensely serious hard sell—that the Odells arrived with their distinctive, often ironic humor: HE PLAYED / A SAX / HAD NO B. O. / BUT HIS WHISKERS SCRATCHED / SO SHE LET HIM GO. There was even an occasional note of irreverence toward other advertising: IT'S NOT TOASTED / IT'S NOT DATED / BUT LOOK OUT / IT'S IMITATED. The little signs first startled, then delighted, the highway traveler. Their unwillingness to be portentous, their amiable iconoclasm,

18

pleased people in the same way that *Ballyhoo* magazine briefly caught the national fancy, or that *Mad* magazine has recently charmed the young. The signs did not shout, and the only odors mentioned were pleasing ones: HIS FACE WAS SMOOTH / AND COOL AS ICE / AND OH LOUISE! / HE SMELLED / SO NICE. There was also an impious absurdity that was captivating, for no advertisers had ever spoken to us this way before: DOES YOUR HUSBAND / MISBEHAVE / GRUNT AND GRUMBLE / RANT AND RAVE / SHOOT THE BRUTE SOME / BURMA-SHAVE. There was unexpectedness about these flippant new signs; one would cruise a familiar highway and come upon, newly installed, a series such as: THE ANSWER TO / A MAIDEN'S / PRAYER / IS NOT A CHIN / OF STUBBY HAIR.

One aspect to the signs not evident at first was that several special advantages were concealed in an arrangement of six small messages planted one hundred paces apart. At 35 miles an hour it took almost three seconds to proceed from sign to sign, or eighteen seconds to march through the whole series. This was far more time and attention than a newspaper or magazine advertiser could realistically expect to win from casual viewers. Yet Burma-Shave almost automatically exacted this attention from virtually every literate passerby; as Alexander Woollcott once observed, it was as difficult to read just one Burma-Shave sign as it was to eat one salted peanut. Once the Odells had taught us that their signs were constructed with a jingling cadence, and were frosted with a topping of folk humor, we grew addicted to a degree that few advertisers have ever achieved for their copy.

Another advantage lay hidden in the spaced-out signs: they established a controlled reading pace, and even added an element of suspense. The eye could not race ahead and anticipate or spoil the effect, as it could on a printed page. Instead the arrangement, like the bouncing ball in a movie group-singing short, concentrated attention on one sign at a time, building effects for the pay-off line, which was usually the fifth. The result was to deliver the message in much the style of a practiced raconteur who sets the stage for his snapper: PITY ALL / THE MIGHTY CAESARS / THEY PULLED / EACH WHISKER OUT / WITH TWEEZERS. Concentrating the effect in the fifth line was not simply a story-telling device; it also had echoes from childhood and even infancy when, perhaps to avert the threatened approach of bedtime, we begged (just once more) for a favorite rhyme or song: THE BEARDED LADY / TRIED A JAR / SHE'S NOW / A FAMOUS / MOVIE STAR.

Curious and wonderful results, unprecedented in the history of advertising, developed from these hidden characteristics of the six-line highway jingle. One was that people soon developed favorites, reading them aloud with even more savor than the first time they were encountered. The entire carload would chant as if a litany: BENEATH THIS STONE / LIES ELMER GUSH / TICKLED TO DEATH / BY HIS / SHAVING BRUSH. With many families the privilege of reading Burma-Shave signs aloud was a rotated honor, leading inevitably to sharp contention ("It is *so* my turn!"). There was also often someone assigned the duty of peering backward to capture and unscramble the signs that faced in the other direction, a task that required quick wit and a good memory: OF THEM FOR SEED / TO LEAVE ONE HALF / YOU DON'T NEED / WHISKERS / WHEN CUTTING.

Certain themes recurred through all the Burma-Shave jingles, like a motif for a French horn echoing through a symphony. One was the accept-no-substitutes theme. Substitution is an idea that eats corrosively into the mind of advertisers, most particularly those whose products are retailed in groceries and drugstores. The idea is embittering, like a plot from Greek tragedy: one has spent

20

money in building up a demand, and a customer wanders in off the street, maybe not having the name of The Product just right, and then a wretched clerk foists off on him a jar of The Competition, and all that fine money has gone to waste, and, worse, The Competition has rung up a sale, and is even started down the road of earning Product Loyalty for the stuff. It is a nightmare that can make advertisers writhe, and the Odells were no exception. But where conventional, printed-media advertisers would exhort Accept No Substitutes, making virtually no effect whatever on the glazed or unseeing eyes of their readers, the Odells contrived even here a note of gaiety: GIVE THE GUY / THE TOE OF YOUR BOOT / WHO TRIES / TO HAND YOU / A SUBSTITUTE. The intensity of hostility felt toward errant clerks is reflected in another jingle: THE GAME LAWS / OUGHT TO / LET YOU SHOOT / THE BIRD WHO HANDS YOU / A SUBSTITUTE. Occasionally one could detect a resolute effort to take a calm and rational view toward the matter: LET'S GIVE THE / CLERK A HAND / WHO NEVER / PALMS OFF / ANOTHER BRAND. A goaded-beyond-endurance patience was reflected this way: SUBSTITUTES / WOULD IRK A SAINT / YOU HOPE THEY ARE / WHAT YOU KNOW / THEY AIN'T.

The selling of a brushless shaving cream required the changing of settled habits. Gramps and Father had both used a badger-hair brush and perhaps a specially marked shaving mug; why should one change a time-honored and, indeed, traditionally masculine rite? Allan Odell approached the problem from a variety of ways: convenience, modernity, speed, improved results, and the elimination of a need, when traveling, to pack a wet brush. Sometimes the competitive arguments were graphic. Noting the growing acceptance of electric shavers, Clinton Odell himself tossed off a humdinger: A SILKY CHEEK /

SHAVED SMOOTH / AND CLEAN / IS NOT OB-
TAINED / WITH A MOWING MACHINE.

It was almost inevitable that competitive arguments
inched close to the edge of propriety. For years Clinton
recalled with wry amusement what happened when he,
perhaps nodding for an instant, had approved a slightly
distasteful jingle. As luck would have it, the jingle was
installed directly across from a fashionable and dignified
church in suburban Minneapolis. Bright new signs chanted
the message SHAVING BRUSH / ALL WET / AND
HAIRY / I'VE PASSED YOU UP / FOR SANITARY
/ BURMA-SHAVE. On the Sunday following the appearance of these unfortunate words, a party of stony-
faced deacons assembled, marched across the street in
their formal garb, and bodily plucked the motes from
their eye.

Hairy brushes were by no means the sole competitors.
Also striving for the favor of whiskery U.S. males were
three other major brushless preparations, Mollé, Krank's
Shave Cream, and Barbasol. Further, as soon as it grew

apparent that the creams were making inroads into the overall market, what the trade called the Big Soapers—Colgate, Palmolive, Williams, and the rest—promptly began to sell brushless creams of their own. And in the depression years, dozens of private brands appeared in the drug chains and the "pine board" (discount) stores. Being manufactured by regional cosmetic companies and bearing higher profit margins for retailers, these private brands added special meaning to Allan's preoccupation with substitution. In the heat of competition there would sometimes be a flash of tooth at the breezy little upstart. At one point Barbasol brandished its lawyers ominously over the jingle lines NO BRUSH / NO LATHER / NO RUB-IN. It was alleged that these words were the exclusive property of Barbasol, as evidenced by the nightly caroling over the American airwaves of the theme song of Singin' Sam, the Barbasol Man. Sam's song was "Barbasol, Barbasol—no brush, no lather, no rub-in—wet your razor and begin." "I don't think they really had a case," said Leonard Odell, "but we didn't bother to

fight them over it. By that time we were jingling so much we didn't need the line."

Procuring an adequate supply of jingles threatened for a time to be a serious problem. (At first they weren't even verses, just advertising admonitions. But as the Odell high spirits took over, and the advantages of rhyme became evident, the basic format was established.) Allan and Clinton composed all copy for the first few years. They gave birth to a few classics, notably EVERY SHAVER / NOW CAN SNORE / SIX MORE MINUTES / THAN BEFORE, and another of the early great ones: HALF A POUND / FOR / HALF A DOLLAR / SPREAD ON THIN / ABOVE THE COLLAR. Yet by the end of the Twenties it was painfully evident that their muse was growing haggard and scrawny. After a brief and unpromising dalliance with staff "jingle artists," Allan turned to the idea of an annual contest, with $100 paid for each verse accepted. When entries poured in by the thousands, it became excitingly clear that, thanks to industrious versifiers all over the country, the Burma-Shave muse was not only rejuvenated but, indeed, more fetching than ever.

Leonard Odell explained the contest mechanisms this way: "We were out for the best jingles we could get. Each year we advertised the contest over the radio, in magazines and newspapers, and in syndicated Sunday comic sections. We also made sure that people who had previously submitted winners were reminded of the new contest. At the beginning Dad was the principal screener. He'd go up to our summer camp with thousands of entries—we'd send more up to him each day—and for three or four weeks he'd scratch out the ones that had no possibilities, or that might have offended people. Then all of us would whittle away at his preliminary selection.

"After a while it got to be too much for Dad; some of the contests drew more than fifty thousand entries. We hired a couple of experts, women who worked as ad-

24

agency copywriters, to come in for a few weeks and filter out the best ones. They were darned good at it, too, once they got the hang of it. Not all of the entries were clean; it was hard to believe that people would sit down and write the things they did. Anyhow, after they'd picked the top thousand, we'd make copies of them for the company officers and the board of directors. Each of us would pick the twenty or twenty-five best, and we'd meet and find out that we'd picked different ones, and then the arguments began. We had a whale of a lot of fun—much more than in most directors' meetings. But we also took them very seriously, because jingles were our bread and butter. We'd just keep thinning them down, going back for more readings, trading favorites with each other, and meeting again. Sometimes it took us several weeks to agree on the next crop."

Quite naturally the disputations often turned on matters of taste. THE OTHER WOMAN / IN HIS LIFE / SAID "GO BACK HOME / AND SCRATCH YOUR WIFE" was regretfully vetoed for highway use, as was another on a reciprocal theme: MY MAN / WON'T SHAVE / SEZ HAZEL HUZ / BUT I SHOULD WORRY / DORA'S DOES. As senior officer, Clinton Odell served as a kind of Horatius at the bridge, vigilantly defending the American highway against anything off-color or scatological. LISTEN, BIRDS / THESE SIGNS COST / MONEY / SO ROOST A WHILE / BUT DON'T GET FUNNY had strong advocacy in committee, although it was never used. Another near miss: THE WIFE OF BRISTLY / BRUSHMUG ZAYMER / BOUGHT TWIN BEDS / WHO CAN BLAME HER?

Possibly one reason why these disputations arose was an awareness in the boardroom that the certified clean, boy-girl jingles were near the core of the most memorable Burma-Shave verse: SAID JULIET / TO ROMEO / IF YOU WON'T SHAVE / GO HOMEO. Often it was amiably suggested that Burma-Shave could facilitate courtship: WITH / A SLEEK CHEEK / PRESSED TO HERS / JEEPERS! CREEPERS! / HOW SHE PURRS. The same remedy was also prescribed for luckless males who didn't know any girls: HIS FACE / WAS LOVED / BY JUST HIS MOTHER / HE BURMA-SHAVED / AND NOW—— / OH, BROTHER! The grim possibility of a loveless life was sketched in one cautionary

26

lyric: BACHELOR'S QUARTERS / DOG ON THE RUG / WHISKERS TO BLAME / NO ONE / TO HUG. A record of persistent failure with females might be accounted for this way: TO GET / AWAY FROM / HAIRY APES / LADIES JUMP / FROM FIRE ES-CAPES.

Perhaps the all-time classic among boy-girl jingles, however, was a compact and metrically memorable verse from 1934. For reasons beyond easy analysis, it appears to have become engraved on the collective American memory: HE HAD THE RING / HE HAD THE FLAT / BUT SHE FELT HIS CHIN / AND THAT / WAS THAT.

4:

Don't Stick
Your Elbow
Out so Far

Leafing through a list of old Burma-Shave jingles is
also to leaf through almost unrecalled memories and as-
sociations. Suddenly you are driving to Maine again in that
hot summer of 1932 and your companion, a radiant girl
who is now a grandmother, is delighted north of Portland
to come upon FOR PAINTING / COW-SHED / BARN
OR FENCE / THAT SHAVING BRUSH / IS JUST
IMMENSE. Or the half-recollected fact that the Burma-
Shave people devoted many signs to the cause of highway
safety comes back with a rush at the sight of REMEMBER
THIS / IF YOU'D / BE SPARED / TRAINS DON'T
WHISTLE / BECAUSE THEY'RE SCARED.

Public service, as it happened, was one of the major
themes recurring in the complete canon. Two other
themes, Allan Odell once told an advertising trade journal,
are "straight advertising and exaggerated humor." Another
way of putting it would be to classify the jingles as being
either product advertising or public-service advertising,
each category being served up in tones that ranged from
the reasonably serious to the wildly rib-poking. And no
matter how much the first five signs devoted themselves
to the public weal, that sixth one always mentioned the

AT SHAVING BRUSH   IS JUST IMMENSE   Burma-Shave

product. It was notable, in fact, that we were nationally conditioned to put it in even if it wasn't there, as various other advertisers who attempted to imitate the serial format ruefully discovered.

The first public-service jingle appeared in 1935, written by Allan. It managed deftly to combine a safety admonition with a plug for the product: KEEP WELL / TO THE RIGHT / OF THE ONCOMING CAR / GET YOUR CLOSE SHAVES / FROM THE HALF-POUND JAR. In 1937 a woman in Nebraska contributed a tersely macabre thought: DRIVE / WITH CARE / BE ALIVE / WHEN YOU / ARRIVE. In 1938 a man in Wichita received $100 for a lyric that would later recur in variant forms: DON'T TAKE / A CURVE / AT 60 PER / WE HATE TO LOSE / A CUSTOMER. The following year the safety theme came on strong, used in six of the twenty-one new jingles planted along the highways for 1939.

The moving force behind this trend was Clinton Odell. "Dad felt that we'd grown to be a part of the U.S. roadside," Leonard explained, "and had a duty to do what we could about the mounting accident rate. He figured that if people would remember our humorous messages,

31

they just might have more effect than routine do-this, don't-do-that safety advice. And of course we always had our name at the end of each set." It was a shrewd policy also in that it established the firm as being public-spirited, an attitude that could only be an asset in confronting the ominously growing anti-billboard forces. Throughout the country, regulation, special taxes, and outright prohibition of road signs were spreading; and it befitted Burma-Shave, which almost alone among businesses was solely dependent on road signs, to cultivate the reputation of being helpful as well as cheerful.

Several of that first large crop in 1939 managed to effect a jaunty tone with what could scarcely have been described as a droll theme. Wrote a woman from Illinois: HARDLY A DRIVER / IS NOW ALIVE / WHO PASSED / ON HILLS / AT 75. From Michigan came a variation on the hate-to-lose-a-customer concept: PAST / SCHOOLHOUSES / TAKE IT SLOW / LET THE LITTLE / SHAVERS GROW. (A decade later the idea was retooled this way: AT SCHOOL ZONES / HEED INSTRUCTIONS! / PROTECT / OUR LITTLE / TAX DEDUCTIONS.) Sardonic advice arrived from a New Jerseyite: AT CROSSROADS / DON'T JUST / TRUST TO LUCK / THE OTHER CAR / MAY BE A TRUCK.

The following year the number of highway-safety jingles had risen to seven out of twenty-two. The feat of linking shaving cream and highway safety was managed, at slight metric cost, by a Philadelphian who composed: ALWAYS REMEMBER / ON ANY TRIP / KEEP TWO THINGS / WITHIN YOUR GRIP / YOUR STEERING WHEEL AND / BURMA-SHAVE. As was perhaps inevitable, the boundary between the catchy and the grim was not easily established. Observed one plain-speaking lady: WHEN YOU DRIVE / IF CAUTION CEASES / YOU ARE APT / TO REST / IN PIECES. A distinctly gloomy prediction came from Indiana: DON'T PASS CARS /

32

PAST

SCHOOLHOUSES

TAKE IT SLOW

LET THE LITTLE

SHAVERS GROW

Burma-Shave

ON CURVE OR HILL / IF THE COPS / DON'T GET YOU / MORTICIANS WILL. A lady from Shamrock, Texas, won her $100 with a Cassandra-like forecast: DON'T STICK / YOUR ELBOW / OUT SO FAR / IT MIGHT GO HOME / IN ANOTHER CAR.

The basic problem was beautifully stated in a 1942 jingle: DROVE TOO LONG / DRIVER SNOOZING / WHAT HAPPENED NEXT / IS NOT / AMUSING. In time a variety of devices were used to adapt the somber aspects of safety to the genial Burma-Shave format. One such device was to employ the boy-girl theme so successful with other jingles: IF HUGGING / ON HIGHWAYS / IS YOUR SPORT / TRADE IN YOUR CAR / FOR A DAVENPORT. Or as a poet from the Southwest noted: TRAINS DON'T WANDER / ALL OVER THE MAP / FOR NO ONE / SITS ON / THE ENGINEER'S LAP. A matron of Birmingham, Alabama, evidently a spiritual daughter of La Rochefoucauld, composed what was clearly more an epigram than a jingle: A GIRL / SHOULD HOLD ON / TO HER YOUTH / BUT NOT / WHEN HE'S DRIVING.

A second adaptive device was to use Pearly-Gates imagery, for here familiarity from long use by humorists and cartoonists had leached away the grimness: AT INTERSECTIONS / LOOK EACH WAY / A HARP SOUNDS NICE / BUT IT'S HARD TO PLAY. From a lady of Issaqua, Washington, came this thought: GUYS WHOSE EYES / ARE IN THEIR BACKS / GET HALOS CROSSING / RAILROAD TRACKS.

Puns and wordplay, another Burma-Shave staple, also helped: HE SAW / THE TRAIN / AND TRIED TO DUCK IT / KICKED FIRST THE GAS / AND THEN THE BUCKET. Yet puns proved as unreliable for the Burma-Shave versifiers as they have been for the rest of mankind, being sometimes fine and sometimes ghastly: HER CHARIOT / RACED AT 80 PER / THEY

HAULED AWAY / WHAT HAD / BEN HUR. It was in fact with puns that the Burma-Shave editorial taste, ordinarily so finely attuned to the highway readership, proved sometimes uncertain: TRAIN APPROACHING / WHISTLE SQUEALING / PAUSE! / AVOID THAT / RUN-DOWN FEELING!

It would be inaccurate, however, to suggest that the overtones of highway safety gave serious problems to most jinglers. Often they selected naturally undistressing hazards: TWINKLE, TWINKLE / ONE-EYED CAR / WE ALL WONDER / *WHERE* / YOU ARE. A woman of Illinois earned $100 with her blithe inquiry: IS HE / LONESOME / OR JUST BLIND / THIS GUY WHO DRIVES / SO CLOSE BEHIND? Drunken driving came in for full attention, once with an intricate multiple pun: DRINKING DRIVERS / NOTHING WORSE / THEY PUT THE QUART / BEFORE THE HEARSE.

But trouble can lie in wait for the unwary, however well intentioned. In 1948 a jingle announced: THE MIDNIGHT RIDE / OF PAUL / FOR BEER / LED TO A / WARMER HEMISPHERE. No sooner was this rather undistinguished lyric erected about the country than a scorching letter arrived on the desk of the Burma-Shave board chairman. It was from a national association of beer haulers, and its gist, as the Odells recall, was "Doggone it, we've got about forty-one jillion members, and if you don't get that set of signs off the road pronto you're going to start losing a lot of customers, because beer-haulers shave just like everybody else." Since Clinton's policy was never to give offense, the midnight ride of Paul for beer disappeared as rapidly as the crews could replace it. Safety was furthered equally well by jingles that mentioned no commercial products: AROUND / THE CURVE / LICKETY-SPLIT / IT'S A BEAUTIFUL CAR / WASN'T IT?

The actual value of the highway-safety jingles was inherently unmeasurable, although it must have been substantial. A sheaf of praising letters and testimonials from safety officials and highway commissioners collected in the office, pleasing Clinton Odell greatly. He was also delighted to hear of a study on average highway speeds conducted by the University of Pennsylvania; it reported parenthetically that no phenomenon more reliably slowed down speeders than a set of Burma-Shave signs. This behavior was reflected in a 1955 jingle: SLOW DOWN, PA / SAKES ALIVE / MA MISSED SIGNS / FOUR / AND FIVE.

As Clinton interpreted it, public service extended beyond highway safety. A number of jingles on the prevention of forest fires were erected during the Fifties, spotted in locations where they could do the most good. Although of surely commendable intent, it was interesting and perhaps significant that they lacked the expected Burma-Shave zest: MANY A FOREST / USED TO STAND / WHERE A / LIGHTED MATCH / GOT OUT OF HAND. Something of this slightly devitalized quality had been evident earlier. In the months following Pearl Harbor, a number of sequences exhorting citizens to purchase bonds were quickly tooled up, and it was notable that they were marked more by laudable patriotism than by memorable concept and phrase: LET'S MAKE HITLER / AND HIROHITO / LOOK AS SICK AS / OLD BENITO / BUY DEFENSE BONDS. However, by evoking boot camps, basic training, and weekend passes, the main-line jingles quickly captured the essential Burma-Shave spirit: "AT EASE," SHE SAID / "MANEUVERS BEGIN / WHEN YOU GET / THOSE WHISKERS / OFF YOUR CHIN."

5:

The Way
It Worked

FIDELIA M. DEARLOVE, for thirty-three years Allan
Odell's secretary, did most of the paperwork on the road
signs, and it was considerable. From her route lists, files,
and pin-bristling maps, she could almost always tell what
jingle was located where, when it had been inspected last,
when the agreement with the farmer or landholder would
expire, and when the crew in a truck would be along
to change copy to a sprightly new verse. With nearly
seven thousand sets amounting to forty thousand individual signs scattered from Maine to Texas, and with
twenty to twenty-five new jingles being installed regularly
to replace an equal number already out, Miss Dearlove
had a complex, ever changing situation to keep track of.
What made it especially difficult was its dynamic quality:
each day there would be mail or phoned reports from an
advance man or the crews of installers on the road—
they began in the south in winter and fanned out north
as the weather bettered—reporting on departures from the
original plan, or on new local sign taxes or other circumstances. It was no wonder that when some question about
signs came up, almost everyone in the home office had
the instinctive reaction of "ask Fidelia."

In the decade following the appearance of those first
primitive signs on the roads to Albert Lea and Red Wing,
Burma-Shave verses began to sprout like wildflowers. By
the fall of 1926, with $25,000 spent on signs, they were
dotted through Minnesota, Wisconsin, and Iowa; and
sales had grown from virtually zero to about $68,000.
In 1927, with an advertising appropriation of $45,000,
signs had spread through most of the rest of the Midwest,
and sales doubled. By 1929, with $65,000 spent on signs,
the first exploratory tongues had reached both the At-
lantic and Pacific coasts, with sales doubling once again.
In 1930 the signs diffused through the South and New
England. Carl Noren, risen to serving as a director of

the Burma-Vita Company, was able to say with comfortable precision that "we never knew that there was a depression." During its peak times the company grossed more than $3,000,000 a year, demonstrating the greater effectiveness of cheerful jingles over the door-to-door appeal of Jars on Approval.

The only states that the roadside signs never formally appeared in were Arizona, Nevada, and New Mexico—deemed to have insufficient traffic density—and Massachusetts, deemed to present such obstacles as winding roads, excessive and obscuring foliage, and insufficient numbers of reasonably priced locations.

The first portent of a Burma-Shave invasion into new territory was the sight of the advance man, assigned to buy locations. He'd cruise along main, through highways, watching for spots that met his requirements: a straight and fairly level stretch, at road height, or no more than three or four feet lower, never higher. A place bearing other signs was to be avoided, particularly big billboards that could eclipse part of a series. The site should be visible for a considerable distance, it having been found that, if the set began just after a curve, some people would miss the first sign or two, an annoyance sufficient, in some cases, to generate testy letters of complaint.

Once a likely spot was identified, the advance man (who, like so many others connected with Burma-Shave, was likely to have a hearty, friendly personality) would approach the farmer owning the land, present him with a jar of the product, show him a sign, and begin negotiations: "How'd you like to have a set of these signs put up along the fence there?" This may not always have been the ideal opener, for it was recorded that exceptionally rustic farmers were known to counter warily: "How much is it going to cost me?" But in general a mutually agreeable deal could be concluded without difficulty, a year's lease of rights to install and maintain the signs

39

bringing the farmer from five to twenty-five dollars, depending on the desirability of the location. Occasionally a David Harum who owned a particularly choice spot, and who was resistant to the marked friendliness of the advance man, might get fifty dollars or even more a year, although such cases were rare.

Renewals were handled by mail; Fidelia worked out a system of sending out new contracts well in advance of expiration. If a farmer balked at signing, displaying inflated ideas of the site's value, she simply instructed a truck crew to remove the signs at their next passage. Mostly the relationship between farmers and Burma-Shave was an amiable one, with many leases extending for decades. "Oh, occasionally we'd get a man who'd pull down some signs to patch up his barn," noted John Kammerer, head of the company sign shop, "but it was mainly all the other way. The farmers were kind of proud of those signs. They'd often write us if a sign had become damaged, asking us to ship a replacement that they'd put up themselves. In the years when we brought old signs back here to the plant, when lumber was short, I'd sometimes see where they had repaired or repainted signs on their own hook, often doing a fine job of it, too."

Once the advance man had signed up the farmer, the two would pace off the location, tying bright strips of red or orange cloth to the fence to signal the spot for the installation crew following along behind. The crew, traveling in a 1½-ton truck jauntily painted with such admonitions as Cheer Up, Face, the War Is Over, would typically be manned by several husky Minnesota youngsters, appropriately muscled for the assignment of digging thirty-six postholes per day, each one no less than three feet deep. According to carefully fostered rumor, any indolent lad who found that digging to this depth through stubborn shale or past heavy boulders was excessively fatiguing, and who therefore covertly sawed off a foot or eighteen inches from the *bottom* of the post, was liable to summary discharge.

The company displayed a characteristic old-shoe informality in its sign operations. Periodic attempts to systematize it—special regional crews, a complex pattern of leaving trucks and gear in storage in remote parts of the country—were tried and discarded. Instead, the firm settled in to an informal but effective pattern. The dozen or so people in the sign shop, having pitched in during the cruelest part of the Minnesota winter to start production on the new crop of signs and having shipped off the first few hundred sets to regional warehouses, would then divide up in part to set out on the highways. They would be subdivided into several advance men, traveling solo, and three or four truck-borne pairs of installers, laden with signs and equipment, and all bearing Fidelia's latest route maps. With almost the dedication of Crusaders or seekers of the Holy Grail, they would often set out at the end of February and not return home to Minnesota until the ground froze around Thanksgiving. Each truck bore about forty sets of signs, perhaps six or seven working days' supply, after which it was necessary to put in at a regional warehouse and load up again.

There was much informal doubling of duties. The advance man would circle back after signs had been up in a new territory for a few weeks, paying sales calls on drugstores and wholesalers, and usually discovering that a pleasing demand had been generated. The muscular young installers—whom the Odells were accustomed to describe as qualified PhDs, the letters standing for Posthole Diggers—were also often pressed into service as the nucleus of a crew of "samplers," busily handing out small free tubes or jars at ball games, wrestling matches, and other convocations of males.

"We made a few mistakes," noted Burdette Booth, a shyly friendly man who has worked for Burma-Shave

43

all his life. "Once in Los Angeles I had a crew giving out sample jars to men as they filed in to a wrestling match. Then everybody got mad at one of the wrestlers, and they started pitching those jars into the ring—they were just like *rocks,* perfect for throwing—and it was a wonder no one got klonked. After that I learned to sample as people were coming out of a gathering, not as they went in." In New York Leonard Odell learned the same lesson when a crew of his passed out sample tubes of Burma-Shave to baseball fans entering Ebbets Field. After the plate umpire made a call unfavorable to the Dodgers, much of the infield became so densely carpeted with tubes of brushless shaving cream that it was necessary to suspend play until the groundskeepers could tidy up.

Booth, who has served as installer, advance man, salesman, sampler, and plant engineer during his thirty-four years with the company, remembers each assignment as being a lot of fun, in different ways. "Of course you were away from home for long stretches. If I knew I'd be in an area for a while my wife would join me and we'd get a furnished room somewhere. Ohio was one state that I worked over real hard; I put up more than seven hundred sets of signs there. That could be real work—digging postholes all day long. Sometimes when you came back to the cabin or motel after work, people would see the truck painted Cheer Up, Face, and they'd say 'So *you're* the Burma-Shave man!' They sort of thought of you as the Good Humor man, and expected you to be comical on the spot, which was not always easy with an aching back."

The signs themselves underwent continuous evolution. For the first five years they were one-inch pine boards, ten inches high and a yard long, dip-painted twice with the background color mixed with preservative. The lettering, a standard sign painter's Gothic, was applied by silk screen. Letters were four inches high unless the line doubled, when they were squeezed to three and one-fourth inches. To emphasize the new crop of jingles, signs alternated by years between red with white lettering and orange with black lettering. Signs were bolted to steel posts nine feet long. Depending on the length of the location, they were installed ten to twenty yards apart, usually inside the farmer's fence or stone wall. Since highway rights-of-way were narrow in the late Twenties, the signs were usually set back only fifteen or twenty feet from the road's edge.

But times have a way of changing. In 1931 the Odells hired John Kammerer, a young Minneapolis sign and silk-screen expert, to look into a little problem they were having in the paint shop with "bleeding, weeping, and running." The little problem was soon licked, but Kam stayed on for thirty-four years, absorbed in experimenting with and improving the signs. Learning that the steel posts rusted out prematurely in wet ground and near the coasts, Kam had them replaced with pressure-treated wood posts that did fine. Then it was noted that signs had a way of disappearing completely on dark nights if they were located near college towns. These depredations were greatly reduced after Kam had the boltholes counter-bored so that the nuts could be unscrewed only with a special wrench, and after he had crosspieces fitted to the bottoms of the posts as anchors. It was still quite possible for an energetic and larcenous lad to decorate his quarters with a Burma-Shave sign, but he now needed more tools and effort than would normally be brought to an impulse theft.

As roads grew wider and cars went faster, Kam and his crew worked steadily to keep up. In stages over the years the signs grew to twelve and then eighteen inches high and to forty inches in width, with corresponding increase of letter height. Posts were located farther back from the highway, as much as forty or fifty feet from the center line. And the distance between signs steadily lengthened until they were planted, the location permitting, as much as fifty yards apart.

Yearly alterations of color had seemed a good way to call attention to the new signs, but it was noticed that whenever people spoke of Burma-Shave signs, they invariably described them as red and white. Orange-and-black ones seem to have made no impression whatever on the public's retina, or at least on its memory. At this the company gave up, going almost exclusively to red and white. It made things simpler, especially as the early pattern of an annual change became increasingly difficult and expensive with thousands of sets of signs scattered around the country. So the company settled into a custom of inspecting each set each year, but replacing it only every other year.

Simplification was an excellent goal because, the company noted, things tended in general to get steadily more complicated. Several states passed laws taxing each working side of a sign, and since the words *Burma-Shave* normally appeared on the reverse of every sign, the tax load in these states abruptly doubled. The response was a special series of "bareback" signs. Again, South Dakota had a law reserving the color red for danger signs; another special series of white-on-blue signs was created for Fidelia's South Dakota route list, which also included part of Minnesota. And again, high taxes on signs and the growing scarcity of good locations, especially on the close-in approaches to such potentially lucrative concentrations of shavers as New York City, San Francisco, and Los Angeles, made the standard six-sign highway set relatively inefficient. For these troublesome roads the response was a special crop of bobtailed signs. They used three, two, or only one board, and the copy usually settled for a single rhyme or pun:

GOOD TO THE LAST STROP

COVERS A MULTITUDE OF CHINS
PAYS DIVIDENDS IN LADY FRIENDS

Still the basic six-sign set, freighted with puns and outrageous humor, remained spread over the American heartland. Experience accumulated for the sign shop and the installers. It was found, for example, that skunks, beavers, and woodchucks were generally less of a nuisance than college boys, although infrequently some rodent with an atypical taste for creosoted wood would gnaw down a sign. Cows as a rule made good neighbors, except that crews would sometimes find where cows had ruminatively rubbed the posts to a bright shine, tilting the set slightly askew in the process. Hunters, who appear to have an uncontrollable tendency to bag all highway signs, perforated many a Burma-Shave set, although usually with small effect. "One nice thing about a pine board," observed Kam recently, "is its ability to absorb gunfire. A drawback to the aluminum signs that we experimented with for a time was that bullet holes were much more conspicuous than with wood. Of course if a youngster with a twelve-gauge shotgun blasted away from a distance of ten feet, it wouldn't do any sign much good."

In the first decades the strangest natural enemies of Burma-Shave signs were horses. Signs in fields where horses were pastured would be found broken off forcibly at the attachment point. Although several jingles referred pejoratively to horses (e.g., OLD DOBBIN / READS THESE SIGNS / EACH DAY / YOU SEE, HE GETS / HIS CORN THAT WAY), the broken signs did not represent literary criticism. Study by Kam and his crew revealed that the signs were being installed at a perfect height to serve as horse back-scratchers. Throughout the country enterprising horses were discovering that, by sidling under an overhanging sign and humping slightly,

47

a richly sensuous scratching could be achieved; and often, in some transport of equine ecstasy, the sign would snap. A partial remedy, quickly instituted, was to use ten-foot posts in place of nine-footers. It is not recorded how horses felt about this deprivation, although the damage was substantially decreased. A combination of uneven ground and tall, enterprising horses allowed it still to happen on occasion, but, as Kam noted a little sadly, "Our horse problem disappeared as, in fact, horses themselves disappeared from American farms. Tractors don't itch."

6:

Free—Free
A Trip to Mars

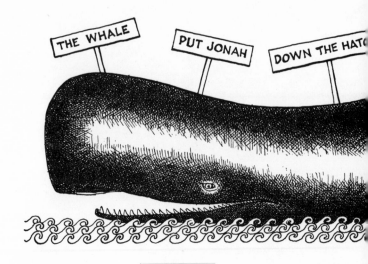

SELLING SHAVING CREAM by jingle may have been an odd way to make a living, but it had its compensations. For one thing, the mail was full of surprises, and Clinton Odell's don't-offend-people dictum meant that all complaints, however odd, had to be judiciously considered. Not all complaints were acted on, though. THE WHALE / PUT JONAH / DOWN THE HATCH / BUT COUGHED HIM UP / BECAUSE HE SCRATCHED drew criticism for irreverence as well as indelicacy, but the signs stayed up. On the other hand, to ease problems of lettering space for Kam's signs, a little simplified spelling was employed experimentally—e.g., *tonite, thot, sez*—but it took only a few reprimands in the mail from English teachers to bring that to a speedy end. And a minor classic of the Thirties, NO LADY LIKES / TO DANCE / OR DINE / ACCOMPANIED BY / A PORCUPINE, although it seemed wholly innocuous, drew an inflamed reproof composed on the letterhead of the Porcupine Club of Boston. We'll have you *know,* the executive secretary wrote in thin-lipped indignation, that

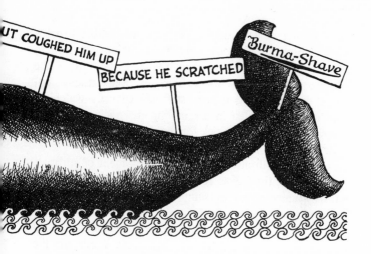

our fraternal organization gives *frequent* dances, attended by ladies who give *every* evidence of *enjoying* themselves. To Leonard Odell fell the task of sending a soothing response. After assurances of exceptional respect by the Burma-Vita Company for porcupines everywhere, he explained that in the New York Advertising Club he was personally a member of a subgroup called the Exalted Order of Goats, and that, speaking as an ex-Grand Odor, he had never felt badly about unfortunate references to namesakes. It was a repy that appeared to mollify the Porcupines.

The mail was unpredictable. WITH GLAMOR GIRLS / YOU'LL NEVER CLICK / BEWHISKERED / LIKE A / BOLSHEVIK, appearing in 1940, brought an especially testy complaint. It was postmarked from New York City, with an address from a locality near Union Square. Keep up this sort of thing, it rasped in Humphrey Bogart manner, and the old red herring will *really* get you. Allan held this letter for some days, eyeing it uneasily. It was evidently still on his mind a week later when, returning from lunch, he found a parcel on his desk bearing a similar postmark. As he was opening it gingerly, peering into a corner of its wrapping, he suddenly realized that it ticked ominously. It took only a few strides for him to race to the mixing room down the hall and plunge the package into a tank of water. This reaction virtually convulsed the office and factory staff, all covertly watching, who had collaborated in assembling the package, and in choosing an old alarm clock for the dangerous implications of its tick.

Burdette Booth also remembered a moment of surprise. "We were on the Texas route, changing copy and giving out half-ounce tubes as samples. In Austin we noticed that some cartons of samples were leaking—poor crimping on the tubes, maybe. I phoned Minneapolis and Al said to destroy them. 'Don't just leave them on the dump where someone might find them' he said. So early next morning, in a misty dawn, we stopped the truck on a bridge over a fair-sized river and pitched over the eight or ten leaky boxes. I knew the cartons would come apart and the tubes would sink.

"That afternoon in a town a hundred miles away I was parking the truck when I saw a Texas Ranger in the left-hand mirror. Then I saw another one in the right-hand mirror, and they both had their guns drawn. 'All right' they said, just like Gary Cooper. 'Get out slowly, with your hands high.' They made us unload the whole truck while they inspected the contents. What happened, I found out, was that a housewife had reported seeing two men on the bridge heaving a dismembered body into the river. So the authorities dragged the river but all they found was a piece of carton with *Burma-Shave* on it, and then they radioed out to pick us up. I explained what we'd done. 'All right, but don't do it again' the captain said, and we sure didn't. It's sweaty work unloading the whole truck while hard-eyed guys hold guns on you."

Something about the road-sign operation seemed to invite the unexpected. Leonard recalls a time in the Thirties, posthole-digging his way across New England, when he had just completed the laborious installation of OLD MC DONALD / ON THE FARM / SHAVED SO HARD / HE BROKE HIS ARM / THEN HE BOUGHT / BURMA-SHAVE. He was driving slowly past the signs to check them when he noticed from the mailbox, and verified from Fidelia's route list, that the farmer's name was in fact McDonald. "I didn't know what to do. I figured that we probably ought to take down the whole set, even though it was getting on toward dark. Finally we nervously hunted him up. He was a big man, kind of solemn. When I explained, he just looked at me for a long moment. Then he burst out laughing. Turned out that he got a big kick out of it, and of course the whole neighborhood did too."

In another case a young sailor sent in a long letter. His ship had just returned from an extended training cruise off Alaska, and he wished to relate a most re-markable occurrence, memorable to the several hundred young trainees aboard. They had been steaming above the Aleutians and, the weather being favorable, had passed through the Bering Strait into the Bering Sea. Those off duty had gathered on deck during the passage through the Strait, with Big Diomede Island on the portside and beyond it the mainland of Asia. Ice floes dotted the dark waters. As the ship nosed past a large floe, those on deck were flabbergasted to see a familiar row of small red signs strung along the ice. Binoculars revealed that all but the last sign—which clearly said *Burma-Shave*—were let-tered eerily in the Russian alphabet. One sailor with a smattering of Russian announced that the jingle appeared to make some Cyrillic witticism about polar bears. The ship steamed slowly on, bearing several hundred baffled trainees. It was only later that the explanation circulated through the ship's company: the signs had been planted, as an elaborate but thoroughly rewarding practical joke, by the crew of a helicopter flying ahead on ice reconnaissance.

The friendly relationship between Burma-Shave and the U.S. Navy was reflected later, during Operation Deepfreeze in Antarctica. Would the company care to contribute some signs, the Navy asked gravely, to sustain the morale of the men stationed on that remote subcontinent? Gosh, yes, Allan replied, enclosing a list of the sign sets then available. The three jingles chosen mirrored nicely the circumstances near the South Pole. One set was a public-service admonition on forest fires, and was erected on a road from the airbase at McMurdo Sound some thousand miles from the nearest combustible tree. A second set reflected the generally whiskery state prevailing: DEAR LOVER BOY / YOUR PHOTO CAME / BUT YOUR DOGGONE BEARD / WON'T FIT / THE FRAME.

The third jingle chosen recalled, perhaps wistfully, the fact that human females were not permitted in Antarctica: USE OUR CREAM / AND WE BETCHA / GIRLS WON'T WAIT / THEY'LL COME / AND GETCHA.

It was characteristic of the luck of the Odells that photographs of the last series—erected in a howling wilderness with a snow tractor in the background and five politely interested penguins gracing the foreground—were picked up by United Press International and distributed to scores of U.S. newspapers. Even after allowing for the fact that Burma-Shave had become a sort of national institution, it was evident that Allan and Leonard had a knack for unpaid publicity that Barnum would have envied.

During the great days of radio, hundreds of "mention permissions" were granted to everyone from Amos 'n Andy to Jimmy Durante and Bob Hope. When television bloomed, it was not unnoticed that the signs could be as

visual as the jingles had been oral. Many of the mentions on network air were brief (e.g., said Fibber McGee scornfully, "I've read better poetry than that on Burma-Shave signs with the last two posts missing"), but some were not, as in 1941 when Bob Hope devoted almost fifteen minutes to a Burma-Shave episode. Fred Allen had a particular fondness for gags built around the signs. One night on the Texaco Hour he devoted so much time to a skit titled "The Murder of the Burma-Shave Poet" that the Odells concluded that "we probably got more out of that network broadcast than Texaco did." Requests for permission to mention usually arrived by phone or telegram, with a note of urgency, and everyone in the office, down to the newest secretary, was authorized to issue permission "just so it was clean and wouldn't offend people."

Sometimes it was even possible to exploit a slightly misfiring jingle. In a time when retailing was being deviled by a fad for coupons, Allan wrote a satirical jingle: FREE OFFER! FREE OFFER! ! / RIP A FENDER / OFF YOUR CAR / MAIL IT IN FOR / A HALF-POUND JAR. While some 99 percent of those seeing this jingle interpreted it as satire, or at least as the light-hearted lunacy to be expected from Burma-Shave, the remaining 1 percent constituted a problem in cleanliness and rubbish disposal. Scores of fenders of notable decrepitude arrived at the plant by parcel post and express. Many enterprising people scavenged Minnesota junkyards, triumphantly bearing off rusty horrors that they lugged to the Burma-Shave offices. Others shipped in fenders forcibly detached from toy cars, which at least had the merit of depositing less dirt and rust. Each donor was greeted with simulated polite surprise, and courteously presented with a jar of Burma-Shave. As Leonard observed, it was one of those delightful little things that happen occasionally. Perhaps more to the point, by later relating the anecdote to the press, the Odells reaped far more value in publicity than the worth of the jars given out.

Once, however, the Odells met their match as amateur Barnums. Again the initiating jingle had been written by Allan, in this case the repeat of an earlier spoof: FREE—FREE / A TRIP / TO MARS / FOR 900 / EMPTY JARS. Although this offer seemed safe, the Odells had not reckoned on Arliss French, manager of a supermarket in Appleton, Wisconsin, one of a chain of Red Owl stores. Mr. French, widely known as Frenchy and no mean exploiter himself, took up the challenge with enthusiasm. He wired Burma-Shave that he was accepting their offer and where should the jars be shipped? After a bit of pencil-chewing, Allan wired back: If a trip to Mars you'd earn, remember, friend, there's no return.

But Frenchy was not easily put off; and besides, business in his store was being stirred up gratifyingly. He countered with a second publicized telegram: Let's not quibble, let's not fret, gather your forces, I'm all set. To this the Odells sent an almost obligatory response: Our rockets are ready; we ain't splitting hairs; just send us the jars—and arrange your affairs. They also sent Ralph Getchman, the general manager of Burma-Shave, to Appleton to see just what was going on.

As Leonard remembers it, "Ralph telephoned me soon: 'This boy's serious! He's got big reproductions of our signs running the full length of his store. He's putting full-page ads in the local paper saying Send Frenchy to Mars! In the store he's got jars heaped up in a huge pile. Any time people buy Burma-Shave he empties the cream into an ice-cream carton and keeps the jar. He's got some kind of rocket plane in the store that kids are swarming all over, and he's got little green men on the roof firing toy rocket gliders out over the parking lot.' I told Ralph the best I could think of for the moment was to send him to the Mars Candy Company down in Chicago for a week-end on the town, which was just barely good enough of an idea to get me off the phone.

"Meantime, though, the Red Owl chain was getting a big kick out of it, especially with the way the volume in the store was up. To help Frenchy they hired a publicity man named Moran, a fellow with a big red beard. He came to see us and said that we had a *great* idea going here. He'd discovered that there was a little town in Germany called Mars—spelled Moers actually, but pronounced Mars—population about a hundred and twenty-two, near Düsseldorf. He said that if we'd pay the plane fare, he'd take care of the rest, and that's how we did it. We decided to send Mrs. French along too, figuring that since she had eleven or twelve children maybe she could use a little vacation.

"So Frenchy showed up here with a bubble on his head, dressed in a silvery space suit with a big red owl on the front. They rented a Brink's armored truck to deliver the jars; it had a big sign on it, Sending Frenchy to Mars. We gave him some full jars that he could use in Mars to barter for goods and services. It made quite an affair for the TV and news photographers. The Frenches spent the night in Al's house, and he drove them to the airport in the morning. In Mars there was a three-day festival that was a dilly, with dancing in the streets and people coming in for miles around. The Frenches had a marvelous time, and when they got home they wrote us a wonderful letter. We still get Christmas cards from them.

"It was a real fun kind of thing," Leonard Odell concluded. "And syndicated right across the country."

7:

An End
to the
Road Signs

THE LITERARY QUALITY of the Burma-Shave verse was highly variable, not surprising, perhaps, considering that even Shakespeare did not attempt seven hundred sonnets. A minority of the jingles were—there is no other word for it—appalling: PEDRO / WALKED / BACK HOME BY GOLLY / HIS BRISTLY CHIN / WAS HOT-TO-MOLLY. Every now and then one moved beyond gaiety toward agitation: HE ASKED / HIS KITTEN / TO PET AND PURR / SHE EYED HIS PUSS / AND SCREAMED "WHAT FUR!" A few skirted the limits of felicity: HE LIT A MATCH / TO CHECK GAS TANK / THAT'S WHY / THEY CALL HIM / SKIN-LESS FRANK. There was, finally, a taste for the kind of whimsy that can sweep like a breeze across a grammar-school playground: HIS BRUSH IS GONE / SO WHAT'LL WE DO / SAID MIKE ROBE I / TO MIKE ROBE II.

At times numerous observers (including the Odells themselves) have dismissed the jingles as corny. This is an easy if not notably discerning assessment. Disregarding an occasional deviation, the jingles were in total a remarkable potpourri of folk humor, wit, and skillfully offbeat merchandising. While to dissect is sometimes to destroy, it is nevertheless possible to isolate certain of the elements that produced such generally pleasing and popular effects.

One characteristic, partly enforced by the format, was conciseness—an attribute that has been broadly popular from Aesop through Poor Richard to the fad for Confucius Say. The shortest full-sized jingle of record needed only seven words for its safety admonition: FROM / BAR / TO CAR / TO / GATES AJAR. Another notable compaction was: BROKEN ROMANCE / STATED FULLY / SHE WENT WILD / WHEN HE / WENT WOOLY.

Humor was, obviously, the second important characteristic. Those who undertake to analyze the complete canon will find that at least seven different strains of humor were employed. One was punning and wordplay, often enhanced by the serial effect: MY JOB IS / KEEPING FACES CLEAN / AND NOBODY KNOWS / DE STUBBLE / I'VE SEEN. Another was pure slapstick, in the mainstream of Buster Keaton and Red Skelton: SHE KISSED / THE HAIRBRUSH / BY MISTAKE / SHE THOUGHT IT WAS / HER HUSBAND JAKE. A pseudo-proverb was a favorite device, effective because the sententiousness associated with apothegms set up a nice contrast: WITHIN THIS VALE / OF TOIL / AND SIN / YOUR HEAD GROWS BALD / BUT NOT YOUR CHIN. (This jingle, incidentally, was a special favorite of the Odells'.) An irritable if not waspish wit was often used with telling effect, as in this highway-safety note: DON'T LOSE / YOUR HEAD / TO GAIN A MINUTE / YOU NEED YOUR HEAD / YOUR BRAINS ARE IN IT. The flirty-but-clean sex theme mentioned earlier was good for many a giggle, as was the use (rare among road signs) of topical themes: WE DON'T / KNOW HOW / TO SPLIT AN ATOM / BUT AS TO WHISKERS / LET US AT 'EM. Lastly, the sardonic and quietly sharp tongue often heard in country stores was basic: EVERY DAY / WE DO / OUR PART / TO MAKE YOUR FACE / A WORK OF ART.

A graduate-school dissertation recently prepared by George Odell, Allan's son, *The Burma-Vita Company and Its Relationship to Twentieth Century America,* makes a number of subtle observations about the corpus of the jingles. Their humor, George Odell notes, was often based on the image of the whisker, a concept faintly ludicrous to begin with, and certainly not as repulsive as many other drugstore advertising images. There was also the typically Western humor of exaggeration: WE'VE MADE / GRANDPA / LOOK SO TRIM / THE LOCAL / DRAFT BOARD'S AFTER HIM. This wide-swinging extravagance, traceable back past Mark Twain, Josh Billings, and Bret Harte, found sympathetic responses everywhere west of the Mississippi. The consistent use of slang and colloquialism, George Odell wrote, was comforting to viewers; it was reassuring to find a chatty, familiar jingle on a road many miles from home. Almost inevitably the impression was given that the company sure must be made up of friendly plain folks, very different from those other advertisers of drugstore products, who noisily threatened malodorousness, disease, and decay.

* * *

The commercial fortunes of the Burma-Vita Company can be read like tea leaves in the jingles themselves. For most of the first twenty years the company had at least one jingle per crop that engagingly bragged about the increased number of users. In 1947 came this spirited cock-a-doodle-doo: ALTHO / WE'VE SOLD / SIX MILLION OTHERS / WE STILL CAN'T SELL / THOSE COUGHDROP BROTHERS. But from then on there were notes of strain. In 1948, writing in a house organ called *The Burma Sign Post,* Allan reported slightly decreasing sales and greatly increasing costs, with company officers taking cuts in salary. Other omens followed. The bragging jingle of 1955 showed no increase: 6 MILLION HOUSEWIVES / CAN'T BE WRONG / WHO KEEP / THEIR HUSBANDS / RIGHT ALONG IN / BURMA-SHAVE.

This seven-year plateau was hardly promising in a time of national expansion. Other evidences piled up: increased re-use of existing, bought-and-paid-for rhymes; a tendency to choose the more hard-selling among these; a sharp drop in the ratio of public-service jingles; and then, most ominous of all, a four-year hiatus in which no new jingles whatever were erected. Although it was not visible from the texts of the verses, these were years in which the company was experimenting with alternative methods of advertising, such as radio and TV, as well as with economies of sign manufacture and maintenance.

Clearly the sales magic was slowly draining out of the sprightly little red signs. There were as many explanations as explainers. People were driving too fast to read small signs. Or the fun had gone out of the jingles themselves. Or it was all the fault of the superhighways with their sprawling rights-of-way and frequent exclusion of all commercial signs. Or it was urban growth and associated suburban spraddle. (Despite huge sampling drives, bus and car cards, and special signs on the feeder routes, large cities were a continuing problem that the Burma-Shave strategists never solved satisfactorily. This failure was serious because important marketing areas of the country were turning into supercities, accreting together more each year, like globules and curds on a slowly spreading puddle.)

Some mandarins of advertising had, quite naturally, a lucid if self-serving explanation: homemade, corny little signs, produced without benefit of agency commission, were no longer enough; now it was vital to portray graphically why the product was superior to its competitors, as by TV demonstrations. An opinion-polling marketing analyst made a depth study that was festooned with impressive garlands of statistical theory; the corporate image and possible future of Burma-Shave that emerged dimly from the welter of decimal places was, as is the custom with such studies, made up of equal parts of encouragement, discouragement, and enigma. Allan himself had a terser verdict: "Times change. If we were starting over now, I'm not sure the idea would work today."

It should not be thought that the Burma-Vita Company

had any intention of lurching blindly into bankruptcy. Impressive numbers of males were still purchasing jars, tubes, and their new aerosol siblings. Modest sidelines of after-shave and pre-electric lotions, deodorants, and even a tooth powder were adding to the gross. There was the memory of a mosquito repellent that had been discontinued only after a singularly mosquito-free summer, and a line of razor blades that had done just fine until the war had cut off supplies of adequate steel. Instead, the difficulty lay in the managerial implications of the situation: there were clear evidences that the road signs were not only growing costlier (some $200,000 a year by the 1960s) but also steadily less effective. Plainly it was expedient to divert more and more of this money into such standard advertising media as print, radio, and TV; and less of it into the fine goofy old road signs that had built and nourished the business.

This dreary if prudent course was already in effect when, on February 7, 1963, it was announced publicly that the Burma-Vita Company had been sold to Philip Morris, Inc. It would become an operating division of a subsidiary, American Safety Razor Products. Allan Odell, for fifteen years president and treasurer of Burma-Vita and in a sense its major creator, chose to enter semi-retirement although he would serve the new entity as a consultant; his younger brother Leonard would act as president of the new division. The two brothers were no longer young; and their father, Clinton, had died in 1958 at the age of eighty. "We were the last of the original Big Four to sell out," Leonard noted recently. The sale was a major milestone on the route that had begun, thirty-eight years before, on the road to Red Wing.

The Odells' decision to reduce gradually the number of road signs, replacing them with other advertising media, was ratified by the new owners. The action was, in fact, accelerated. It was determined that all signs were to be taken down as soon as practicable. One couldn't simply leave them up to fade into picturesque decay; and besides, counsel were of the opinion that if the signs stayed up, one might be held to continue to owe farmers rent money. So the trucks—still painted Cheer Up, Face—were sent out for the last time, fanning across the country on Fidelia Dearlove's routes. Crews unbolted the anti-college-boy attachment points and uprooted the posts, so that nothing visible remained of what had been. Only where the posts were so firmly embedded that extraction was virtually impossible did the crews saw them off flush with the ground, leaving the prescribed three feet of depth buried like an invisible marker. Farmers often seemed sad at the removal, and not just because of the cessation of rent checks. "It's sort of like losing an old friend," crews were told.

Characteristically, Allan and Leonard made the most of the elegaic spirit implied in such comment. Scores of newspaper feature writers and columnists proved eager to do pieces about the demise of Burma-Shave road signs; editorial writers fell into a mood of *Eheu! fugaces;* and the *Saturday Evening Post* ran a beautifully crafted article by William K. Zinsser that was later re-used in the *Reader's Digest*. At the Advertising Club of New York, a well-touted luncheon (with a jingle briefly erected outside along the dignified center mall of Park Avenue) was held for the joint purposes of saying farewell to the signs and of introducing Miss Nobu McCarthy, a Eurasian actress of exceptional charm hired to make Burma-Shave TV commercials. In general, farewells to the signs grew into a promotion that quite dwarfed such earlier triumphs as torn-off fenders and Frenchy's weekend in Mars.

It was also evident that all this was eyed with a certain tart envy within advertising and promotion circles; comment in the trade press noted that the Odells had "set off a wave of nostalgia" and that the "signs were having

as many retirements as an aging opera star." Probably the prevailingly wary attitude toward the Odells was most nicely expressed in 1964 by a man from the Washington *Star*. He described Leonard as a "genial, talkative man of fifty-seven with a highly suspect hayseed air. 'I'm just a country boy,' he will say disarmingly, but there is something about him that makes a city slicker count his fingers after a handshake."

On this occasion Leonard was in Washington to give a set of signs to the Smithsonian. The cultural-history section of that institution, alerted and possibly alarmed by all the publicity about the disappearance of the signs, had requested a typical set. After some thought the Odells chose their favorite about your-head-grows-bald-but-not-your-chin for permanent preservation. (There was, needless to say, no hesitancy about passing over hot-to-Molly or skinless Frank.) The presentation made a fine news story, and was comforting to all connected with the company. It remained for George Odell, Allan's son, to point out the special irony of preserving in the Smithsonian the advertising device of a firm that, in an earlier day, had plastered the country with: SHAVING BRUSHES / YOU'LL SOON SEE 'EM / ON THE SHELF / IN SOME / MUSEUM.

A question is often raised today as to whether the Burma-Shave road signs are actually all gone. Perhaps it is a quirk of memory or some persistence of vision, but many people will assure an inquirer that a set was noticed just a few weeks ago on the road to Chambersburg, or maybe it was that straight stretch just south of Winthrop. So far as is known, this is an illusion, a memory in masquerade. (Yet with some thirty-five thousand individual signs once planted about the nation, it is certainly not impossible for a few to have evaded the dismantling crews; so the chance of a few spectral sets, picked up in the headlights of certain older cars on misty nights, should perhaps not be wholly discounted.) But to the knowledge of the Burma-Vita Company, the only signs in existence today outside the factory are those donated to museums, or given to friends and gracing winding private driveways, and a few that have turned up, bearing outrageous price tags, in enterprising antique shops.

The question of the physical existence of a possible handful of remaining signs is scarcely worth a search program. Unlike the annual count of whooping cranes, this census would in the end be like one conducted to count the passenger pigeon or the great auk. More meaningful, perhaps, is the fact that the little red signs still exist, very much alive, in thousands of memories. The setting in each case is individual, although the memories

67

have much in common. It may be that you are en route to Shady Grove by Pine Lake, driving a spunky Ford V-8 or a delightful Packard with bright red hexagons on its hubcaps. The sun is high, the sky blue, and drifting into the open car there is the warm tar smell from the road, blended with new honeysuckle. Then along the roadside this cadenced message unfolds:

> IF YOU
> DON'T KNOW
> WHOSE SIGNS
> THESE ARE
> YOU CAN'T HAVE
> DRIVEN VERY FAR.

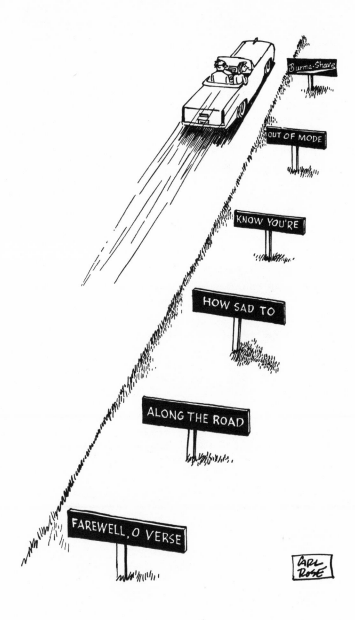

Appendix:

Texts of All
Burma-Shave
Signs

It HAS BEEN SAID that the most carefully perfected plan for the cataloging of a heterogeneous body of objects can never be more than partially satisfactory, and this is eminently true of the Burma-Shave jingles. The listing below, prepared from the company's own records and thus as complete and exact as is possible today, nevertheless presents various technical difficulties to a compiler. The Burma-Vita Company, although expert in the manufacture and sale of shaving cream, had neither a trained historian nor an archivist, and their records present several problems:

1. Texts of the very first sets of homemade signs, placed experimentally on the roads to Red Wing and Albert Lea, are lost. Testimony of participants indicates, however, that the texts used in 1927 were slight elaborations of the originals—i.e., that the earliest texts are contained within the 1927 series.

2. Variant forms of a number of jingles occurred when they were subsequently re-used. The commonest change was to revise the division of words among signs, but textual revision was not unknown. Note for example that in the "museum" jingle of 1930 the line *Way down East* recurs later as *On the shelf*.

3. Records on special jingles for regional tests or for such regionally marketed products as tooth powder, blades, or lotion were not always detailed. The special bobtailed jingles employed on the approaches to certain cities in 1939 and later are not identified by year of use, and were not always changed in annual or biennial cycles.

Finally, a note about editing. The texts here presented are precisely those in company records, shown unaltered. Changes made have been limited to the elimination of authors' names and addresses, of incomplete notations of sign colors used, and of identifying code numbers. F.H.R. Jr.

1927

SHAVE THE
    MODERN WAY
NO BRUSH
NO LATHER
NO RUB-IN
BIG TUBE 35¢
    DRUG STORES
BURMA-SHAVE

GOODBYE!
    SHAVING BRUSH
HALF A POUND
    FOR
HALF A DOLLAR
VERY FINE
    FOR THE SKIN
DRUGGISTS HAVE IT
CHEER UP FACE
    THE WAR IS OVER
BURMA-SHAVE

1928

HOLLER
HALF A POUND
    FOR
HALF A DOLLAR
OH BOY!
SHAVING JOY
COMPLEXION SAVE
BURMA-SHAVE

SHAVE THE MODERN WAY
WASH THE FACE
APPLY WITH FINGERS
SHAVE
BIG TUBE 35¢
BURMA-SHAVE

TAKES THE "H"
    OUT OF SHAVE
MAKES IT
    SAVE
SAVES COMPLEXION
SAVES TIME & MONEY
NO BRUSH
    NO LATHER
BURMA-SHAVE

ONE OF THE
    GREAT DISCOVERIES
GOODBYE! SHAVING
    BRUSH
OLD MEN LOOK YOUNGER
YOUNG MEN LOOK
    HANDSOMER
VERY FINE FOR THE SKIN
BURMA-SHAVE

1929

EVERY SHAVER
NOW CAN SNORE
SIX MORE MINUTES
THAN BEFORE
BY USING
BURMA-SHAVE

YOUR SHAVING BRUSH
HAS HAD ITS DAY
SO WHY NOT
SHAVE THE MODERN WAY
WITH
BURMA-SHAVE

```
TWO                          HALF A POUND
HUNDRED                      FOR
THOUSAND                     HALF A DOLLAR
MEN                          SPREAD ON THIN
USE                          ABOVE THE COLLAR
BURMA-SHAVE                  BURMA-SHAVE
```

1930

```
ONE POUND      85¢           DOES YOUR HUSBAND
HALF POUND     50¢           MISBEHAVE
BIG TUBE       35¢           GRUNT AND GRUMBLE
DON'T PUT IT OFF             RANT AND RAVE
PUT IT ON                    SHOOT THE BRUTE SOME
BURMA-SHAVE                  BURMA-SHAVE


SHAVING BRUSHES              EARLY TO BED
SUCH A BOTHER                EARLY TO RISE
BURMA-SHAVE                  WAS MEANT FOR THOSE
LOOKS GOOD                   OLD FASHIONED GUYS
TO                           WHO DON'T USE
FATHER                       BURMA-SHAVE


BE                           UNCLE RUBE
NO                           BUYS TUBE
LONGER                       ONE WEEK
LATHER'S SLAVE               LOOKS SLEEK
TREAT YOURSELF TO            LIKE SHEIK
BURMA-SHAVE                  BURMA-SHAVE


THO STIFF                    SHAVING BRUSHES
THE BEARD                    YOU'LL SOON SEE 'EM
THAT NATURE GAVE             WAY DOWN EAST
IT SHAVES LIKE DOWN          IN SOME
WITH                         MUSEUM
BURMA-SHAVE                  BURMA-SHAVE


FIVE                         CHEER UP FACE
HUNDRED                      THE WAR IS PAST
THOUSAND                     THE "H" IS OUT
MEN                          OF SHAVE
USE                          AT LAST
BURMA-SHAVE                  BURMA-SHAVE
```

HALF A POUND
FOR
HALF A DOLLAR
AT THE DRUG STORE
SIMPLY HOLLER
BURMA-SHAVE

SHAVING BRUSHES
YOU'LL SOON SEE 'EM
ON THE SHELF
IN SOME
MUSEUM
BURMA-SHAVE

SIX
HUNDRED
THOUSAND
MEN
USE
BURMA-SHAVE

1880 A.D.
STRAIGHT RAZOR AND
SHAVING SOAP
1930 A.D.
SAFETY RAZOR AND
BURMA-SHAVE

THE 50¢ JAR
SO LARGE
BY HECK
EVEN THE SCOTCH
NOW SHAVE THE NECK
BURMA-SHAVE

ARE YOUR WHISKERS
WHEN YOU WAKE
TOUGHER THAN
A TWO-BIT STEAK?
TRY
BURMA-SHAVE

MODERN MAN
SPREADS IT ON
PATS IT IN
SHAVES IT OFF
SEE HIM GRIN
BURMA-SHAVE

BUY A TUBE
USE IT ONE WEEK
IF YOU THEN WANT
YOUR MONEY BACK
SEND US THE TUBE
BURMA-SHAVE

HINKY DINKY
PARLEY VOO
CHEER UP FACE
THE WAR
IS THRU
BURMA-SHAVE

1931

EIGHT
HUNDRED
THOUSAND
MEN
USE
BURMA-SHAVE

TAKE A TIP
FOR YOUR TRIP
NO WET BRUSH
TO SOAK
YOUR GRIP
BURMA-SHAVE

74

FILM PROTECTS
YOUR NECK
AND CHIN
SO YOUR RAZOR
WON'T DIG IN
BURMA-SHAVE

THE ONE HORSE SHAY
HAS HAD ITS DAY
SO HAS THE BRUSH
AND LATHER WAY
USE
BURMA-SHAVE

IT'S A GOOD
OLD SPANISH CUSTOM
TAKE YOUR MUG
AND BRUSH
AND BUST 'EM
BURMA-SHAVE

NO MATTER HOW
YOU SLICE IT
IT'S STILL YOUR FACE
BE HUMANE
USE
BURMA-SHAVE

HELLO DRUGGIST
I DON'T MEAN MAYBE
YES
SIR!
THAT'S THE BABY
BURMA-SHAVE

HALF A POUND
FOR
HALF A BUCK
COME ON SHAVERS
YOU'RE IN LUCK
BURMA-SHAVE

GOLFERS!
IF FEWER STROKES
ARE WHAT YOU CRAVE
YOU'RE OUT OF THE
    ROUGH
WITH
BURMA-SHAVE

THO TOUGH
AND ROUGH
FROM WIND AND WAVE
YOUR CHEEK GROWS
    SLEEK
WITH
BURMA-SHAVE

SHAVING BRUSH
ALL WET
AND HAIRY
I'VE PASSED YOU UP
FOR SANITARY
BURMA-SHAVE

MAKES SHAVING
A
GRIN GAME
NOT
A SKIN GAME
BURMA-SHAVE

1932

POLITICAL PULL
MAY BE
OF USE
FOR RAZOR PULL
THERE'S NO EXCUSE
BURMA-SHAVE

LISTEN SHAVERS
KNOCK ON WOOD
WHEN OFFERED
SOMETHING
"JUST AS GOOD"
BURMA-SHAVE

75

_____(HEBREW)
_____(CHINESE)
_____(GREEK)
THE BEST SHAVE
IN ANY LANGUAGE
BURMA-SHAVE

A SHAVE
THAT'S REAL
NO CUTS TO HEAL
A SOOTHING
VELVET AFTER-FEEL
BURMA-SHAVE

THE CANNONEERS
WITH HAIRY EARS
ON WIRY WHISKERS
USED TIN SHEARS
UNTIL THEY FOUND
BURMA-SHAVE

THE TUBE'S
A WHOPPER
35 CENTS
EASY SHAVING
LOW EXPENSE
BURMA-SHAVE

BARGAIN HUNTERS
GATHER 'ROUND
FIFTY CENTS
BUYS
HALF A POUND
BURMA-SHAVE

FROM NEW YORK TOWN
TO PUMPKIN HOLLER
IT'S HALF A POUND
FOR
HALF A DOLLAR
BURMA-SHAVE

FREE
ILLUSTRATED
JINGLE BOOK
IN EVERY
PACKAGE
BURMA-SHAVE

YOU'LL LOVE YOUR WIFE
YOU'LL LOVE HER PAW
YOU'LL EVEN LOVE
YOUR MOTHER-IN-LAW
IF YOU USE
BURMA-SHAVE

FOR PAINTING
COW-SHED
BARN OR FENCE
THAT SHAVING BRUSH
IS JUST IMMENSE
BURMA-SHAVE

GIVE THE GUY
THE TOE OF YOUR BOOT
WHO TRIES
TO HAND YOU
A SUBSTITUTE FOR
BURMA-SHAVE

WHEN THE JAR
IS EMPTY
WIFE BEGINS
    TO SING
"FOR SPICES, JAM & JELLY
THAT JAR IS JUST
    THE THING"
BURMA-SHAVE

LAWYERS, DOCTORS
SHEIKS AND BAKERS
MOUNTAINEERS AND
    UNDERTAKERS
MAKE THEIR BRISTLY
    BEARDS BEHAVE
BY USING BRUSHLESS
BURMA-SHAVE

SEVERAL MILLION
MODERN MEN
WILL NEVER
GO BACK
TO THE BRUSH AGAIN
BURMA-SHAVE

1933

MOONLIGHT
AND ROSES
WHISKERS
LIKE MOSES
JUST DON'T GO TOGETHER
BURMA-SHAVE

THE MILLIONTH MAN
HAS JOINED
OUR RANKS
OF HAPPY SHAVERS
MANY THANKS!
BURMA-SHAVE

TRAVELERS!
ALL
YOU NEED IS
A RAZOR
AND
BURMA-SHAVE

LATE RISERS!
SHAVE IN JUST
2 MINUTES FLAT
KISS YOUR WIFE
GRAB YOUR HAT
BURMA-SHAVE

LITTLE SHAVERS
DON'T OVERLOOK
ILLUSTRATED
JINGLE BOOK
IN EVERY PACKAGE
BURMA-SHAVE

IT'S NOT TOASTED
IT'S NOT DATED
BUT LOOK OUT—
IT'S IMITATED
INSIST ON
BURMA-SHAVE

SHAVING BRUSH
WAS LIKE
OLD ROVER
WHEN HE DIED
HE DIED ALL OVER
BURMA-SHAVE

WISE OLD SANDY
SHOPPED AROUND
THIS IS WHAT
OLD SANDY FOUND
50¢ BUYS HALF A POUND
BURMA-SHAVE

THE ANSWER TO
A MAIDEN'S
PRAYER
IS NOT A CHIN
OF STUBBY HAIR
BURMA-SHAVE

SHAVING BRUSH
DON'T YOU CRY
YOU'LL BE A
SHOE DAUBER
BY AND BY
BURMA-SHAVE

WITHIN THIS VALE
OF TOIL
AND SIN
YOUR HEAD GROWS BALD
BUT NOT YOUR CHIN—USE
BURMA-SHAVE

EVERYTHING
IN IT
IS FINE
FOR THE
SKIN
BURMA-SHAVE

BRIDGE PRIZE
FOR MEN
JUST HALF A BUCK
TRY IT, HOSTESS
CHANGE YOUR LUCK
BURMA-SHAVE

RUDDY CHEEKS
AND FACE
OF TAN
NEATLY SHAVEN
WHAT A MAN!
BURMA-SHAVE

MUG AND BRUSH
OLD ADAM
HAD 'EM
IS YOUR HUSBAND
LIKE ADAM, MADAM?
BURMA-SHAVE

TO SHAVING BRUSH
I NEED
NOT CLING
I WILL NOT HUSH
OF THEE I SING
BURMA-SHAVE

FREE OFFER!
    FREE OFFER! !
RIP A FENDER
OFF YOUR CAR
MAIL IT IN FOR
A HALF-POUND JAR
BURMA-SHAVE

HE PLAYED
A SAX
HAD NO B.O.
BUT HIS WHISKERS
    SCRATCHED
SO SHE LET HIM GO
BURMA-SHAVE

THRIFTY SHAVERS
NOW ARE FOUND
BUYING SHAVES
BY THE POUND
ONE LB. JAR 85¢
BURMA-SHAVE

IF YOUR HUBBY
TRUMPS YOUR ACE
HERE'S SOMETHING
THAT WILL
SAVE HIS FACE
BURMA-SHAVE

(Regional Contest, 1933)

25 PRIZES
EVERY WEEK
THRUOUT THE FOOTBALL
    SEASON
YOU'LL FIND YOU'D
    RATHER
USE NO LATHER
B'GOLLY THERE'S A
    REASON
BURMA-SHAVE

78

PRIZE CONTEST DETAILS
MAY BE OBTAINED
AT FOOTBALL BROADCAST
EVERY SATURDAY
OVER WCCO
BURMA-SHAVE

HIT 'EM HIGH
HIT 'EM LOW
IT'S ACTION ROOTERS
    CRAVE
MILLIONS BOAST—
    MILLIONS TOAST
THE ALL-AMERICAN
    SHAVE
BURMA-SHAVE

HIT 'EM HIGH
HIT 'EM LOW
FOLLOW YOUR TEAM
OVER WCCO
AND WIN A PRIZE
BURMA-SHAVE

THERE'S FOOTBALL IN
    THE AIR
AND PRIZES FOR ALL TO
    SHARE
ACCEPT OUR INVITATION
WCCO'S THE STATION
(MANY PRIZES
GET YOUR SHARE)

1934

HE HAD THE RING
HE HAD THE FLAT
BUT SHE FELT HIS CHIN
AND THAT
WAS THAT
BURMA-SHAVE

THE ANSWER TO
A SHAVER'S DREAM
A GREASELESS
NO BRUSH
SHAVING CREAM
BURMA-SHAVE

EVERY DAY
WE DO
OUR PART
TO MAKE YOUR FACE
A WORK OF ART
BURMA-SHAVE

JONAH TOOK
NO BRUSH
TO MOP HIS FACE
WHERE JONAH WENT
HE NEEDED SPACE
BURMA-SHAVE

YOUR BEAUTY, BOYS
IS JUST
SKIN DEEP
WHAT SKIN YOU'VE GOT
YOU OUGHT TO KEEP
BURMA-SHAVE

WHEN CUTTING
WHISKERS
YOU DON'T NEED
TO LEAVE ONE HALF
OF THEM FOR SEED
BURMA-SHAVE

THE BEARDED LADY
TRIED A JAR
SHE'S NOW
A FAMOUS
MOVIE STAR
BURMA-SHAVE

THE GAME LAWS
OUGHT TO
LET YOU SHOOT
THE BIRD WHO HANDS
    YOU
A SUBSTITUTE
BURMA-SHAVE

79

BACHELOR'S QUARTERS
DOG ON THE RUG
WHISKERS TO BLAME
NO ONE
TO HUG
BURMA-SHAVE

BRISTLY BEARD
OR SILKY FUZZ
JUST SHAVE 'EM BACK
TO WHERE
THEY WAS
BURMA-SHAVE

THO LIVING COSTS
ARE UPWARD BOUND
FOUR BITS
STILL BUYS
HALF A POUND
BURMA-SHAVE

PITY ALL
THE MIGHTY CAESARS
THEY PULLED
EACH WHISKER OUT
WITH TWEEZERS
BURMA-SHAVE

LATHER WAS USED
BY DANIEL BOONE
HE LIVED
A 100 YEARS
TOO SOON
BURMA-SHAVE

BENEATH THIS STONE
LIES ELMER GUSH
TICKLED TO DEATH
BY HIS
SHAVING BRUSH
BURMA-SHAVE

COLLEGE BOYS!
YOUR COURAGE MUSTER
SHAVE OFF
THAT FUZZY
COOKIE DUSTER
BURMA-SHAVE

EVERY SECOND
WITHOUT FAIL
SOME STORE
RINGS UP
ANOTHER SALE
BURMA-SHAVE

THAT "PINK TOOTH-
      BRUSH"
IS A CURSE
BUT THAT PINK RAZOR'S
A DARN SIGHT WORSE
USE
BURMA-SHAVE

NOAH HAD WHISKERS
IN THE ARK
BUT HE WOULDN'T GET
      BY
ON A BENCH
IN THE PARK
BURMA-SHAVE

1935

HIS FACE WAS SMOOTH
AND COOL AS ICE
AND OH LOUISE!
HE SMELLED
SO NICE
BURMA-SHAVE

WATER HEATER
OUT OF KILTER
TRY THE BRUSHLESS
WHISKER
WILTER
BURMA-SHAVE

80

HELPS
YOUR BUDGET
HOLD ITS GROUND
HALF A DOLLAR
HALF A POUND
BURMA-SHAVE

CUTIE INVITED
VARSITY HOP
GUY FULL
OF WHISKERS
PARTY A FLOP
BURMA-SHAVE

DEWHISKERED
KISSES
DEFROST
THE
MISSES
BURMA-SHAVE

IT TOOK YEARS
TO PERFECT
FOR YOU
A BRUSHLESS CREAM
THAT'S GREASELESS TOO
BURMA-SHAVE

WITH 200 KINDS
FROM WHICH TO CHOOSE
2 MILLION MEN
PREFER
TO USE
BURMA-SHAVE

I JUST JOINED
THE YOUNG MAN SAID
A NUDIST CAMP
IS MY FACE RED?
NO! I USE
BURMA-SHAVE

AVOID THE STORE
WHICH CLAIMS
YOU SHOULD
BUY SOMETHING ELSE
THAT'S JUST AS GOOD
BURMA-SHAVE

20 MILES PER GAL.
SAYS WELL-KNOWN CAR
TO GO 10,000
MILES PER GAL
BUY HALF-POUND JAR
BURMA-SHAVE

IF YOU THINK
SHE LIKES
YOUR BRISTLES
WALK BARE-FOOTED
THROUGH SOME THISTLES
BURMA-SHAVE

YOU KNOW
YOUR ONIONS
LETTUCE SUPPOSE
THIS BEETS 'EM ALL
DON'T TURNIP YOUR NOSE
BURMA-SHAVE

GRANDPA'S BEARD
WAS STIFF AND COARSE
AND THAT'S WHAT
CAUSED HIS
FIFTH DIVORCE
BURMA-SHAVE

TUBE
IMMENSE
35 CENTS
EASY SHAVING
LOW EXPENSE
BURMA-SHAVE

KEEP WELL
TO THE RIGHT
OF THE ONCOMING CAR
GET YOUR CLOSE SHAVES
FROM THE HALF-POUND
    JAR
BURMA-SHAVE

ENTHUSIASTIC USER
HENRY J. MC LASS
SPREADS OUR PRODUCT
ON THE LAWN
WHEN HE CUTS THE
    GRASS
BURMA-SHAVE

BE A MODERN
PAUL REVERE
SPREAD THE NEWS
FROM EAR
TO EAR
BURMA-SHAVE

THE HAPPY GOLFER
FINDS WITH GLEE
THE SHAVE
THAT SUITS HIM
TO A TEE
BURMA-SHAVE

WHISKERS LONG
MADE SAMSON STRONG
BUT SAMSON'S GAL
SHE DONE
HIM WRONG
BURMA-SHAVE

EENY-MEENY
MINY-MO
SAVE YOUR SKIN
YOUR TIME
YOUR DOUGH
BURMA-SHAVE

AT XMAS TIME
AND BIRTHDAYS TOO
WE SOLVE
YOUR PROBLEMS RIGHT
FOR YOU—GIVE
BURMA-SHAVE

SHAVING BRUSH
IS OUT OF DATE
USE THE
RAZOR'S
PERFECT MATE
BURMA-SHAVE

HALF A BUCK
HALF A POUND
NO SUBSTITUTE
IS EVER FOUND
FOR
BURMA-SHAVE

IF SUBSTITUTION
HE SHOULD TRY
JUST LOOK THAT CLERK
RIGHT IN THE EYE
AND BELLOW:
BURMA-SHAVE

1936

RIOT AT
DRUG STORE
CALLING ALL CARS
100 CUSTOMERS
99 JARS
BURMA-SHAVE

TO GET
AWAY FROM
HAIRY APES
LADIES JUMP
FROM FIRE ESCAPES
BURMA-SHAVE

82

SPECIAL TREATMENT
EVERY HAIR
HOLDS IT UP
AND CUTS
IT SQUARE
BURMA-SHAVE

YOUR RAZOR
FLOATS THRU
THE HAIR
WITH THE
GREATEST OF EASE
BURMA-SHAVE

ED'S FACE
IS ROUGH
AND RUGGED
ED'S WIFE
DOESN'T HUG ED
BURMA-SHAVE

SHAVING BRUSH
& SOAPY SMEAR
WENT OUT OF
STYLE WITH
HOOPS MY DEAR
BURMA-SHAVE

TO EVERY MAN
HIS SHAVE
IS BEST
UNTIL HE MAKES
THE FINAL TEST
BURMA-SHAVE

GOLFERS!
HOLE IN ONE
IS QUITE A FEAT
UNLESS THAT HOLE
IS IN YOUR MEAT
BURMA-SHAVE

IF YOU
AND WHISKERS
DO HOBNOB
SOME SAILOR GOB
WILL STEAL YOUR SQUAB
BURMA-SHAVE

IF YOU'RE JUST
AN AVERAGE MAN
WANTING TO LOOK
THE BEST YOU CAN
USE
BURMA-SHAVE

THE CREAM
PRESERVES
PA'S RAZOR BLADE
THE JAR PRESERVES
MA'S MARMALADE
BURMA-SHAVE

FISHERMAN!
FOR A LUCKY STRIKE
SHOW THE PIKE
A FACE
THEY'LL LIKE
BURMA-SHAVE

SMITH BROTHERS
WOULD LOOK IMMENSE
IF THEY'D JUST
COUGH UP 50 CENTS
FOR HALF POUND JAR
BURMA-SHAVE

JIMMIE SAID A
NAUGHTY WORD
JIMMIE'S MOTHER OVER-
HEARD
SOAPSUDS? NO!
HE PREFERRED
BURMA-SHAVE

CONGRESSMAN PIPP
LOST THE ELECTION
BABIES HE KISSED
HAD NO PROTECTION
TO WIN—USE
BURMA-SHAVE

LET'S GIVE THE
CLERK A HAND
WHO NEVER
PALMS OFF
ANOTHER BRAND
BURMA-SHAVE

HIS TENOR VOICE
SHE THOUGHT DIVINE
TILL WHISKERS
SCRATCHED
SWEET ADELINE
BURMA-SHAVE

OLD MC DONALD
ON THE FARM
SHAVED SO HARD
HE BROKE HIS ARM
THEN HE BOUGHT
BURMA-SHAVE

AS YOU JOURNEY
DOWN THE YEARS
YOUR MIRROR IS
THE GLASS THAT CHEERS
IF YOU USE
BURMA-SHAVE

CHEER CHEER
THE GANG'S
ALL HERE
RIDING ALONG
THREE MILLION STRONG
FOR
BURMA-SHAVE

HEAR ABOUT
THE JOLLY TAR
IT SMELLED SO GOOD
HE ATE
A JAR
BURMA-SHAVE

COOTIES LOVE
BEWHISKERED PLACES
CUTIES LOVE THE
SMOOTHEST FACES
SHAVED BY
BURMA-SHAVE

FREE! FREE! !
A TRIP
TO MARS
FOR 900
EMPTY JARS
BURMA-SHAVE

ALL THESE YEARS
YOUR SKIN
HAS DRIED
WHY NOT MOISTEN
UP YOUR HIDE
BURMA-SHAVE

1937

HOLLER!
HALF A POUND
FOR HALF A DOLLAR
ISN'T THAT
A CHEERFUL EARFUL
BURMA-SHAVE

DRIVE
WITH CARE
BE ALIVE
WHEN YOU
ARRIVE
BURMA-SHAVE

84

WEEK-OLD BEARD
SO MASKED HIS FACE
HIS BULL DOG
CHASED HIM
OFF THE PLACE
BURMA-SHAVE

THE CANNIBALS
TOOK JUST ONE VIEW
AND SAID
HE LOOKS TOO NICE
TO STEW
BURMA-SHAVE

LITTLE WILLIE
MODERN SOUL
BUSTED PAPA'S
BRUSH AND BOWL
NICE WORK WILLIE
BURMA-SHAVE

YOU'VE LAUGHED
AT OUR SIGNS
FOR MANY A MILE
BE A SPORT
GIVE US A TRIAL
BURMA-SHAVE

'MID RISING
TAXES
SOARING RENTS
STILL HALF A POUND
FOR FIFTY CENTS
BURMA-SHAVE

IF HARMONY
IS WHAT
YOU CRAVE
THEN GET
A TUBA
BURMA-SHAVE

SUBSTITUTES!
SMOOTH GUYS SELL 'EM
EASY MARKS USE 'EM
WELL GROOMED MEN
ALWAYS REFUSE 'EM
BURMA-SHAVE

THE BURMA GIRLS
IN MANDALAY
DUNK BEARDED LOVERS
IN THE BAY
WHO DON'T USE
BURMA-SHAVE

EVERY
SHEBA
WANTS A SHEIK
STRONG OF MUSCLE
SMOOTH OF CHEEK
BURMA-SHAVE

KIDS! ATTENTION!
44 BEST JINGLES
USED SO FAR
IN JINGLE BOOK
WITH TUBE OR JAR
BURMA-SHAVE

IF *HER* WHISKERS
SCRATCHED *YOUR* CHEEK
YOU WOULD
SEND HER OUT
TO SEEK
BURMA-SHAVE

MEN
WHO'VE TESTED
EVERY BRAND
ARE JUST THE ONES
WHO NOW DEMAND
BURMA-SHAVE

IT'S IN
THE BAG
OF EVERY MAN
WHO TRAVELS
LIGHTLY AS HE CAN
BURMA-SHAVE

FROM SASKATOON
TO ALABAM'
YOU HEAR MEN PRAISE
THE SHAVE
WHAT AM
BURMA-SHAVE

MY NECK WAS SORE
IN FRONT BEFORE
AND ALSO
SORE BEHIND
BEFORE
BURMA-SHAVE

STOMACH ACHE!
DOCTOR—
TOOTHACHE!
DENTIST—
WHISKERS!
BURMA-SHAVE

THE CROWD
YOU SEE
AROUND THAT STORE
ARE BURMA-SHAVERS
BUYING MORE
BURMA-SHAVE

BATHROOM SHELF
SURPRISES ME
FROM SHAVING CLUTTER
IT'S NOW FREE
I'M USING
BURMA-SHAVE

FINGERS WERE MADE
BEFORE BRUSHES—
USE 'EM
THEY'RE MUCH SAFER
YOU CAN'T LOSE 'EM
BURMA-SHAVE

SALESMEN, TOURISTS
CAMPER-OUTERS
ALL YOU OTHER
WHISKER-SPROUTERS
DON'T FORGET YOUR
BURMA-SHAVE

NO PULLING
AT THE WHISKER BASE
A SOOTHING FILM
PROTECTS
YOUR FACE
BURMA-SHAVE

PAPER HANGERS
WITH THE HIVES
NOW CAN
SHAVE WITH
CARVING KNIVES
BURMA-SHAVE

ROMANCES ARE
WRECKED
BEFORE THEY BEGIN
BY A HAIR
ON THE COAT
OR A LOT ON THE CHIN
BURMA-SHAVE

86

"THEY'RE OFF"
HE CRIED
AND FELT HIS CHIN
'TWAS JUST ANOTHER
EASY WIN FOR
BURMA-SHAVE

IF YOU HAVE
A DOUBLE CHIN
YOU'VE TWO
GOOD REASONS
TO BEGIN USING
BURMA-SHAVE

FIRE! FIRE!
KEEP COOL
BE BRAVE
JUST GRAB
YOUR PANTS AND
BURMA-SHAVE

ON A HIGHWAY AD
HE SPIED IT
BOUGHT A JAR
NOW GLAD HE
TRIED IT
BURMA-SHAVE

A SILKY CHEEK
SHAVED SMOOTH
AND CLEAN
IS NOT OBTAINED
WITH A MOWING
    MACHINE
BURMA-SHAVE

RING OUT THE OLD
RING IN THE NEW
WHAT GOOD CAN
SHAVING
BRUSHES DO?
BURMA-SHAVE

CHEEK TO CHEEK
THEY MEANT TO BE
THE LIGHTS WENT OUT
AND SO DID HE
HE NEEDED
BURMA-SHAVE

SAY, BIG BOY
TO GO
THRU LIFE
HOW'D YOU LIKE
A WHISKERED WIFE?
BURMA-SHAVE

HENRY THE EIGHTH
PRINCE OF FRISKERS
LOST FIVE WIVES
BUT KEPT
HIS WHISKERS
BURMA-SHAVE

ARE YOU
AN EVEN-TEMPERED GUY
MAD ALL
THE TIME
BETTER TRY
BURMA-SHAVE

DON'T TAKE
A CURVE
AT 60 PER
WE HATE TO LOSE
A CUSTOMER
BURMA-SHAVE

THE CREAM
ONE HEARS
THE MOST OF NOW
COMES FROM A JAR
NOT FROM A COW
BURMA-SHAVE

THE TIME
TO START
A REAL DISPUTE
IS WHEN YOU'RE
OFFERED A SUBSTITUTE
BURMA-SHAVE

RIP VAN WINKLE
SAID HE'D RATHER
SNOOZE FOR YEARS
THAN SHAVE
WITH LATHER
BURMA-SHAVE

OTHER THINGS HAVE
GONE SKY HIGH
HALF A DOLLAR
STILL WILL BUY
HALF POUND JAR
BURMA-SHAVE

TRAILER FOLK
HAVE LITTLE SPACE
FOR TOTIN' THINGS
TO FIX THE FACE
THEY USE
BURMA-SHAVE

BEFORE I TRIED IT
THE KISSES
I MISSED
BUT AFTERWARD—BOY!
THE MISSES I KISSED
BURMA-SHAVE

(Special Razor Blade
Promotion, 1938)

NO LADY LIKES
TO DANCE
OR DINE
ACCOMPANIED BY
A PORCUPINE
BURMA-SHAVE

AFTER ONE TRIAL
YOU'LL WANT MORE
AT THE NEXT
GOOD DRUG STORE
15 FOR 25¢
BURMA-SHAVE
      BLADES

HERE'S THE WINNING
SHAVING TEAM
THE PERFECT BLADE
THE PERFECT CREAM
BURMA-SHAVE BLADES
BURMA-SHAVE

IN EVERY
HALF A POUND
MY BOY
YOU GET A TON
OF SHAVING JOY
BURMA-SHAVE

SHARPEST BLADE
EVER MADE
COMFORT SPEED
GUARANTEED
15 FOR 25¢
BURMA-SHAVE
      BLADES

HERE'S SOMETHING
THAT COULD
EVEN SOAK
THE WHISKERS OFF
A RADIO JOKE
BURMA-SHAVE

1939

HARDLY A DRIVER
IS NOW ALIVE
WHO PASSED
ON HILLS
AT 75
BURMA-SHAVE

DARLING I AM
GROWING OLD
NONSENSE!
DO AS YOU
ARE TOLD—GET
BURMA-SHAVE

A WHISKERED GENT
AT A BAZAAR
PAID FOR
A KISS
BUT GOT A JAR
BURMA-SHAVE

DRIVE LIKE
A RAILROAD ENGINEER
TAKE IT EASY
WHEN THE ROAD'S
NOT CLEAR
BURMA-SHAVE

MIRROR ON
THE BATHROOM WALL
WHAT'S THE
SMOOTHEST SHAVE
OF ALL?
BURMA-SHAVE

TRY A TUBE
THE CREAM
THAT'S IN IT
IS MAKING FRIENDS
A MAN A MINUTE
BURMA-SHAVE

SOAPS
THAT IRRITATE
THEIR MUGS
TURN JOLLY GENTS
TO JITTERBUGS
BURMA-SHAVE

PAST
SCHOOLHOUSES
TAKE IT SLOW
LET THE LITTLE
SHAVERS GROW
BURMA-SHAVE

MOM AND POP
ARE FEELING GAY
BABY SAID
AS PLAIN
AS DAY
BURMA-SHAVE

IF YOU DISLIKE
BIG TRAFFIC FINES
SLOW DOWN
'TILL YOU
CAN READ THESE SIGNS
BURMA-SHAVE

SHIVER MY TIMBERS
SAID CAPTAIN MACK
WE'RE TEN KNOTS OUT
BUT WE'RE TURNING
    BACK
I FORGOT MY
BURMA-SHAVE

SPECIAL SEATS
RESERVED IN HADES
FOR WHISKERED GUYS
WHO SCRATCH
THE LADIES
BURMA-SHAVE

A PEACH
LOOKS GOOD
WITH LOTS OF FUZZ
BUT MAN'S NO PEACH
AND NEVER WUZ
BURMA-SHAVE

THE QUEEN
OF HEARTS
NOW LOVES THE KNAVE
THE KING
RAN OUT OF
BURMA-SHAVE

SPREAD IT ON
AND LIGHTLY TOO
SHAVE IT OFF
THAT'S ALL
YOU'RE THROUGH
BURMA-SHAVE

AT CROSSROADS
DON'T JUST
TRUST TO LUCK
THE OTHER CAR
MAY BE A TRUCK
BURMA-SHAVE

SHAVING BRUSHES
SOON WILL
BE TRIMMIN'
THOSE SCREWY HATS
WE SEE ON WIMMIN
BURMA-SHAVE

CHRISTMAS COMES
BUT ONCE
A YEAR
ONE SWELL GIFT
THAT'S ALWAYS HERE
BURMA-SHAVE

I PROPOSED
TO IDA
IDA REFUSED
IDA WON MY IDA
IF IDA USED
BURMA-SHAVE

CARELESS DRIVING
SOON WE HOPE
WILL GO
THE WAY
OF BRUSH AND SOAP
BURMA-SHAVE

CARELESS
BRIDEGROOM
DAINTY BRIDE
SCRATCHY WHISKERS
HOMICIDE
BURMA-SHAVE

(These special bobtailed jingles were employed in 1939 and later on the approach routes to a number of large cities, where locattions for full-length jingles were difficult to obtain. Each ended, of course, with the words *Burma-Shave*. They were displayed variously on two or three signs, sometimes even on a single extra-tall board.)

GOOD TO THE LAST STROP

COVERS A MULTITUDE OF CHINS

NIX ON NICKS

FOR FACES THAT GO PLACES

DON'T PUT IT OFF—PUT IT ON

SHAVE FASTER WITHOUT DISASTER

MAKES GOOD BECAUSE IT'S MADE GOOD

TAKES THE "H" OUT OF SHAVE

NO DIGGING IN ON TENDER SKIN

MAKES MISSES MRS.

BRUSH? NO! TOO SLOW

EQUIP YOUR GRIP

NO PUSHEE NO PULLY SMOOTH SHAVY
FEEL BULLY

BEARD UNRULY—MEET YOURS TRULY

AID THE BLADE

THOSE WHO CLICK—PICK

BETTER SHAVING AT A SAVING

START THE DAY THE MODERN WAY

50% QUICKER 100% SLICKER

YOU'LL ENTHUSE AS YOU USE

LOOK "SPIFFY" IN A "JIFFY"

NO SOONER SPREAD THAN DONE

SAVES YOUR JACK—HOLDS YOUR JILL

ROMANCE NEVER STARTS FROM SCRATCH

TRY OUR WHISKER LICKER

JOIN THE MILLIONS USING SOOTHING

A WORD TO THE WIVES IS SUFFICIENT

JUST SPREAD, THEN PAT—NOW SHAVE,
THAT'S THAT!

HOT TIP, PAL—MORE SMILES PER GAL

WON BY A HAIR THAT WASN'T THERE

PAYS DIVIDENDS IN LADY FRIENDS

IS YOUR FACE HER MISFORTUNE? TRY

IF GETTING UP GETS YOU DOWN—USE

WHEN YOU SHOP FOR YOUR POP

ONCE A DAY THE EASY WAY

NO TRICK TO CLICK IF QUICK TO PICK

OTHER DAYS—OTHER WAYS. NOWADAYS

DELUXE DE LOOKS WITH

HE'S NIFTY AND THRIFTY—LOOKS 30 AT 50

BEST REFERENCE—PUBLIC PREFERENCE

ECONOMIZE WITH THIS SIZE

A BETTER BUY—WHY NOT TRY

RIGHT ABOUT FACE

1940

SAID JULIET
TO ROMEO
IF YOU
WON'T SHAVE
GO HOMEO
BURMA-SHAVE

SUBSTITUTES AND
IMITATIONS
SEND 'EM TO
YOUR WIFE'S
RELATIONS
BURMA-SHAVE

WHEN YOU DRIVE
IF CAUTION CEASES
YOU ARE APT
TO REST
IN PIECES
BURMA-SHAVE

HE MARRIED GRACE
WITH SCRATCHY FACE
HE ONLY
GOT ONE DAY
OF GRACE!
BURMA-SHAVE

ALL LITTLE RHYMING
JOKES ASIDE
DON'T BE CONTENT
UNTIL YOU'VE
TRIED
BURMA-SHAVE

COLLEGE CUTIE
PIGSKIN HERO
BRISTLY KISS
HERO
ZERO
BURMA-SHAVE

YOU CAN'T REACH 80
HALE AND HEARTY
BY DRIVING 80
HOME FROM
THE PARTY
BURMA-SHAVE

BUY A JAR
TAKE IT FROM ME
THERE'S SO
MUCH IN IT
THE LAST HALF'S FREE
BURMA-SHAVE

HE'S THE BOY
THE GALS FORGOT
HIS LINE
WAS SMOOTH
HIS CHIN WAS NOT
BURMA-SHAVE

PUT YOUR BRUSH
BACK ON THE SHELF
THE DARN THING
NEEDS A
SHAVE ITSELF
BURMA-SHAVE

IT'S BEST FOR
ONE WHO HITS
THE BOTTLE
TO LET ANOTHER
USE THE THROTTLE
BURMA-SHAVE

DON'T PASS CARS
ON CURVE OR HILL
IF THE COPS
DON'T GET YOU
MORTICIANS WILL
BURMA-SHAVE

WITH GLAMOUR GIRLS
YOU'LL NEVER CLICK
BEWHISKERED
LIKE A
BOLSHEVIK
BURMA-SHAVE

A SCRATCHY CHIN
LIKE BRIGHT
PINK SOCKS
PUTS ANY ROMANCE
ON THE ROCKS
BURMA-SHAVE

ALWAYS REMEMBER
ON ANY TRIP
KEEP TWO THINGS
WITHIN YOUR GRIP
YOUR STEERING WHEEL
AND
BURMA-SHAVE

GIVE HAND SIGNALS
TO THOSE BEHIND
THEY DON'T KNOW
WHAT'S IN
YOUR MIND
BURMA-SHAVE

THE BEARDED DEVIL
IS FORCED
TO DWELL
IN THE ONLY PLACE
WHERE THEY DON'T SELL
BURMA-SHAVE

SUBSTITUTES
WOULD IRK A SAINT
YOU HOPE THEY ARE
WHAT YOU KNOW
THEY AIN'T
BURMA-SHAVE

PRICKLY PEARS
ARE PICKED
FOR PICKLES
NO PEACH PICKS
A FACE THAT PRICKLES
BURMA-SHAVE

GUYS WHOSE EYES
ARE IN
THEIR BACKS
GET HALOS CROSSING
RAILROAD TRACKS
BURMA-SHAVE

A CHRISTMAS HUG
A BIRTHDAY KISS
AWAITS
THE WOMAN
WHO GIVES THIS
BURMA-SHAVE

JUST SPREAD
THEN PAT
NOW SHAVE
THAT'S
THAT
BURMA-SHAVE

1941

HERE'S
A GOOD DEED
FOR A SCOUT
TELL YOUR DAD
ALL ABOUT
BURMA-SHAVE

DON'T STICK
YOUR ELBOW
OUT SO FAR
IT MIGHT GO HOME
IN ANOTHER CAR
BURMA-SHAVE

THEY MISSED
THE TURN
CAR WAS WHIZZ'N
FAULT WAS HER'N
FUNERAL HIS'N
BURMA-SHAVE

SOLDIER
SAILOR
AND MARINE
NOW GET A SHAVE
THAT'S QUICK AND CLEAN
BURMA-SHAVE

TELL
THE DEAR
WHO SHOPS AROUND
THAT HALF A BUCK
BUYS HALF A POUND
BURMA-SHAVE

REMEMBER THIS
IF YOU'D
BE SPARED
TRAINS DON'T WHISTLE
BECAUSE THEY'RE
    SCARED
BURMA-SHAVE

SHE KISSED
THE HAIRBRUSH
BY MISTAKE
SHE THOUGHT IT WAS
HER HUSBAND JAKE
BURMA-SHAVE

WHEN BETTER
SHAVING BRUSHES
ARE MADE
WE'LL STILL SHAVE
WITHOUT THEIR AID
BURMA-SHAVE

HE USED
UMBRELLA
FOR PARACHUTE
NOW REJECTS
EVERY SUBSTITUTE
BURMA-SHAVE

WHEN JUNIOR TAKES
YOUR TIES
AND CAR
IT'S TIME TO BUY
AN EXTRA JAR
BURMA-SHAVE

GETS EACH
WHISKER
AT THE BASE
NO INGROWN HAIR
ON NECK OR FACE
BURMA-SHAVE

THE ANSWER TO
A MAIDEN'S PRAYER
IS A MAN
MOST ANYWHERE
USING
BURMA-SHAVE

IF MAN BITES DOGGIE
THAT IS NEWS
IF FACE
SCARES DOGGIE
BETTER USE
BURMA-SHAVE

RHYME AND REASON
EVERY SEASON
YOU'VE READ
THE RHYME
NOW TRY THE REASON
BURMA-SHAVE

AT INTERSECTIONS
LOOK EACH WAY
A HARP SOUNDS NICE
BUT IT'S
HARD TO PLAY
BURMA-SHAVE

WILD
DASHES
FROM BY-WAYS
CAUSE CRASHES
ON HIGHWAYS
BURMA-SHAVE

LIFE IS SWEET
BUT OH HOW BITTER!
TO LOVE A GAL
AND THEN
NOT GIT 'ER
BURMA-SHAVE

SUBSTITUTES
RESEMBLE
TAIL-CHASING PUP
FOLLOW AND FOLLOW
BUT NEVER CATCH UP
BURMA-SHAVE

TRAINS DON'T WANDER
ALL OVER THE MAP
FOR NO ONE
SITS ON
THE ENGINEER'S LAP
BURMA-SHAVE

FROM
BAR
TO CAR
TO
GATES AJAR
BURMA-SHAVE

WHEN PETER PIPER
PICKLE PICKER
KISSED HIS GAL
HIS BEARD
WOULD PRICK 'ER
BURMA-SHAVE

IF EVERY SIP
FILLS YOU
WITH ZIP
THEN YOUR SIPPER
NEEDS A ZIPPER
BURMA-SHAVE

BROKEN ROMANCE
STATED FULLY
SHE WENT WILD
WHEN HE
WENT WOOLY
BURMA-SHAVE

1942

PA LIKES THE CREAM
MA LIKES THE JAR
BOTH LIKE
THE PRICE
SO THERE YOU ARE
BURMA-SHAVE

STORES ARE FULL
OF SHAVING AIDS
BUT ALL YOU NEED
IS THIS
AND BLADES
BURMA-SHAVE

BROTHER SPEEDERS
LET'S
REHEARSE
ALL TOGETHER
"GOOD MORNING, NURSE!"
BURMA-SHAVE

PA ACTED
SO TICKLED
MA THOT
HE WAS PICKLED
HE'D JUST TRIED
BURMA-SHAVE

'MID RISING
TAXES
SOARING RENTS
STILL HALF A POUND
FOR FIFTY CENTS
BURMA-SHAVE

ICEMAN'S GRANDSON
NOW FULL GROWN
HAS COOLING SYSTEM
ALL HIS OWN
HE USES
BURMA-SHAVE

APPROACHED
A CROSSING
WITHOUT LOOKING
WHO WILL EAT
HIS WIDOW'S COOKING?
BURMA-SHAVE

IF YOU
DON'T KNOW
WHOSE SIGNS
THESE ARE
YOU CAN'T HAVE
DRIVEN VERY FAR

DROVE TOO LONG
DRIVER SNOOZING
WHAT HAPPENED NEXT
IS NOT
AMUSING
BURMA-SHAVE

LET'S MAKE HITLER
AND HIROHITO
LOOK AS SICK AS
OLD BENITO
BUY DEFENSE BONDS
BURMA-SHAVE

CAN'T SHAVE DAILY?
TENDER HIDE?
NOW BE HONEST
HAVE YOU
TRIED
BURMA-SHAVE

THERE'S NO WHISKER
IT WON'T SOFTEN
SHAVE 'EM CLOSE
AND NOT
SO OFTEN
BURMA-SHAVE

IF HUGGING
ON HIGHWAYS
IS YOUR SPORT
TRADE IN YOUR CAR
FOR A DAVENPORT
BURMA-SHAVE

SHAVING BRUSH
IN ARMY PACK
WAS STRAW THAT BROKE
THE ROOKIE'S BACK
USE BRUSHLESS
BURMA-SHAVE

A GIRL
SHOULD HOLD ON
TO HER YOUTH
BUT NOT
WHEN HE'S DRIVING
BURMA-SHAVE

MAYBE YOU CAN'T
SHOULDER A GUN
BUT YOU CAN SHOULDER
THE COST OF ONE
BUY DEFENSE BONDS
BURMA-SHAVE

OF ALL
THE DRUNKS
WHO DRIVE ON SUNDAY
SOME ARE STILL
ALIVE ON MONDAY
BURMA-SHAVE

"AT EASE," SHE SAID
"MANEUVERS BEGIN
WHEN YOU GET
THOSE WHISKERS
OFF YOUR CHIN"
BURMA-SHAVE

SUBSTITUTES
LIKE UNSEEN BARTER
OFTEN MAKE ONE
SAD
BUT SMARTER
BURMA-SHAVE

TRAVELING MEN
KNOW EASE
AND SPEED
THEIR SHAVING KITS
HOLD WHAT THEY NEED
BURMA-SHAVE

WHAT YOU SHOUTED
MAY BE TRUE,
BUT
DID YOU HEAR
WHAT HE CALLED YOU?
BURMA-SHAVE

BUYING DEFENSE BONDS
MEANS MONEY LENT
SO THEY
DON'T COST YOU
ONE RED CENT
BURMA-SHAVE

TO MOST BRUSH SHAVERS
IT'S QUITE CLEAR
THE YANKS AREN'T
        COMING
THE YANKS ARE HERE
USE BRUSHLESS
BURMA-SHAVE

1943

EVERY SHAVER
NOW CAN SNORE
SIX MORE MINUTES
THAN BEFORE
BY USING
BURMA-SHAVE

ONE POUND JAR   85¢
HALF POUND JAR   50¢
BIG TUBE   35¢
DON'T PUT IT OFF
PUT IN ON
BURMA-SHAVE

HALF A POUND
FOR
HALF A DOLLAR
SPREAD ON THIN
ABOVE THE COLLAR
BURMA-SHAVE

SHAVING BRUSHES
YOU'LL SOON SEE 'EM
ON THE SHELF
IN SOME
MUSEUM
BURMA-SHAVE

DOES YOUR HUSBAND
MISBEHAVE
GRUNT AND GRUMBLE
RANT AND RAVE
SHOOT THE BRUTE SOME
BURMA-SHAVE

IT'S A GOOD
OLD SPANISH CUSTOM
TAKE YOUR MUG
AND BRUSH
AND BUST 'EM
BURMA-SHAVE

EARLY TO BED
EARLY TO RISE
WAS MEANT FOR THOSE
OLD FASHIONED GUYS
WHO DON'T USE
BURMA-SHAVE

WITHIN THIS VALE
OF TOIL
AND SIN
YOUR HEAD GROWS BALD
BUT NOT YOUR CHIN—USE
BURMA-SHAVE

SLAP
THE JAP
WITH
IRON
SCRAP
BURMA-SHAVE

THE CANNONEERS
WITH HAIRY EARS
ON WIRY WHISKERS
USED TIN SHEARS
UNTIL THEY FOUND
BURMA-SHAVE

98

FILM PROTECTS
YOUR NECK
AND CHIN
SO YOUR RAZOR
WON'T DIG IN
BURMA-SHAVE

THO TOUGH
AND ROUGH
FROM WIND AND WAVE
YOUR CHEEK GROWS
   SLEEK
WITH
BURMA-SHAVE

1945

MANY A WOLF
IS NEVER LET IN
BECAUSE OF THE HAIR
ON HIS
CHINNY-CHIN-CHIN
BURMA-SHAVE

SHE RAISED CAIN
WHEN HE RAISED
   STUBBLE
GUESS WHAT
SMOOTHED AWAY
THEIR TROUBLE?
BURMA-SHAVE

BIG MISTAKE
MANY MAKE
RELY ON HORN
INSTEAD OF
BRAKE
BURMA-SHAVE

FROM STATISTICS
THAT WE GATHER
THE SWING IS TO
NO BRUSH
NO LATHER
BURMA-SHAVE

NO MAN CAN REALLY
DO HIS STUFF
WITH A FACE THAT'S
   SORE
OR A CHIN
THAT'S ROUGH
BURMA-SHAVE

FIRST MEN BUY IT
THEN APPLY IT
THEN ADVISE
THEIR FRIENDS
TO TRY IT
BURMA-SHAVE

IF THESE
SIGNS BLUR
AND BOUNCE AROUND
YOU'D BETTER PARK
AND WALK TO TOWN
BURMA-SHAVE

THIS IS NOT
A CLEVER VERSE
I TRIED
AND TRIED
BUT JUST
GOT WORSE

YOU CAN BEAT
A MILE A MINUTE
BUT THERE AIN'T
NO FUTURE
IN IT
BURMA-SHAVE

SLEEP IN A CHAIR
NOTHING TO LOSE
BUT A NAP
AT THE WHEEL
IS A PERMANENT SNOOZE
BURMA-SHAVE

LIFE WITH FATHER
IS MORE PLEASANT
SINCE
HE GOT THIS
BIRTHDAY PRESENT
BURMA-SHAVE

IT SPREADS SO SMOOTH
IT SHAVES SO SLICK
IT FEELS
LIKE VELVET
AND IT'S QUICK
BURMA-SHAVE

HIS LINE WAS SMOOTH
BUT NOT HIS CHIN
HE TOOK HER OUT
SHE TOOK HIM IN
TO BUY SOME
BURMA-SHAVE

WHY DOES A CHICKEN
CROSS THE STREET?
SHE SEES A GUY
SHE'D LIKE TO MEET
HE USES
BURMA-SHAVE

TESTED
IN PEACE
PROVEN IN WAR
BETTER NOW
THAN EVER BEFORE
BURMA-SHAVE

TO A SUBSTITUTE
HE GAVE A TRIAL
IT TOOK OFF
NOTHING
BUT HIS SMILE
BURMA-SHAVE

'TWOULD BE
MORE FUN
TO GO BY AIR
IF WE COULD PUT
THESE SIGNS UP THERE
BURMA-SHAVE

DRINKING DRIVERS
ENHANCE THEIR
CHANCE
TO HIGHBALL HOME
IN AN AMBULANCE
BURMA-SHAVE

THE CHICK
HE WED
LET OUT A WHOOP
FELT HIS CHIN AND
FLEW THE COOP
BURMA-SHAVE

BOTH HANDS
ON WHEEL
EYES ON ROAD
THAT'S THE SKILLFUL
DRIVER'S CODE
BURMA-SHAVE

1947

YOU'VE USED
OUR CREAM
NOW TRY OUR BLADES
PAIR UP THE BEST
IN SHAVING AIDS
BURMA-SHAVE

DON'T LOSE
YOUR HEAD
TO GAIN A MINUTE
YOU NEED YOUR HEAD
YOUR BRAINS ARE IN IT
BURMA-SHAVE

100

THAT SHE
COULD COOK
HE HAD HIS DOUBTS
UNTIL SHE CREAMED
HIS BRISTLE SPROUTS
    WITH
BURMA-SHAVE

THE WOLF
WHO LONGS
TO ROAM AND PROWL
SHOULD SHAVE BEFORE
HE STARTS TO HOWL
BURMA-SHAVE

AS YOU DRIVE
PLAY THIS GAME
CONSTRUCT
A JINGLE
WITH THIS NAME
BURMA-SHAVE

IF A GIFT
YOU MUST CHOOSE
GIVE HIM
ONE THAT
HE CAN USE
BURMA-SHAVE

WHEN THE STORK
DELIVERS A BOY
OUR WHOLE
DARN FACTORY
JUMPS FOR JOY
BURMA-SHAVE

JOIN
OUR HAPPY
BRUSHLESS THRONG
SIX MILLION USERS
CAN'T BE WRONG
BURMA-SHAVE

FAMOUS LAST WORDS
OF LIGHTS THAT SHINE
"IF HE WON'T
DIM HIS
I WON'T
DIM MINE"
BURMA-SHAVE

CAR IN DITCH
DRIVER IN TREE
MOON WAS FULL
AND SO
WAS HE
BURMA-SHAVE

SUBSTITUTES
THAT PROMISE
    PERFECTION
ARE LIKE
SOME CANDIDATES
AFTER ELECTION
BURMA-SHAVE

SANTA'S
WHISKERS
NEED NO TRIMMIN'
HE KISSES KIDS
NOT THE WIMMIN
BURMA-SHAVE

ALTHO
WE'VE SOLD
SIX MILLION OTHERS
WE STILL CAN'T SELL
THOSE COUGHDROP
    BROTHERS
BURMA-SHAVE

WE KNOW
HOW MUCH
YOU LOVE THAT GAL
BUT USE BOTH HANDS
FOR DRIVING, PAL
BURMA-SHAVE

101

IN CUPID'S LITTLE
BAG OF TRIX
HERE'S THE ONE
THAT CLIX
WITH CHIX
BURMA-SHAVE

THRIFTY JARS FOR
STAY AT HOMES
HANDY TUBES
FOR HIM
WHO ROAMS
BURMA-SHAVE

I USE IT TOO
THE BALD MAN SAID
IT KEEPS MY FACE
JUST LIKE
MY HEAD
BURMA-SHAVE

GRANDPA'S
OUT WITH
JUNIOR'S DATE
OLD TECHNIQUE
WITH BRAND NEW BAIT
BURMA-SHAVE

NO SOGGY BRUSHES
IN YOUR GRIP
YOU'VE ALWAYS
GOT A
FINGER TIP
BURMA-SHAVE

IF YOU WANT
A HEARTY SQUEEZE
GET OUR
FEMALE
ANTI-FREEZE
BURMA-SHAVE

SUBSTITUTES WOULD
HAVE THEIR PLACE
IF YOU COULD
SUBSTITUTE
YOUR FACE
BURMA-SHAVE

MAN PASSES
DOG HOUSE
DOG SEES CHIN
DOG GETS OUT
MAN GETS IN
BURMA-SHAVE

A GUY
WHO WANTS
TO MIDDLE-AISLE IT
MUST NEVER SCRATCH
HIS LITTLE VIOLET
BURMA-SHAVE

PRICES RISING
O'ER THE NATION
HERE IS ONE
THAT MISSED
INFLATION
BURMA-SHAVE

(Burma-Vita Tooth Powder Jingles)

THE FIRST
IMPROVEMENT
IN MANY A YEAR
FOR CLEANING TEETH
IS FINALLY HERE
BURMA-VITA TOOTH
    POWDER

SPEAKING OF
GREAT EVENTS
BURMA-SHAVE
PROUDLY PRESENTS
ANOTHER FINE PRODUCT
BURMA-VITA TOOTH
    POWDER

102

JUST MOISTEN
YOUR TOOTH BRUSH
DIP IN JAR
AND YOU'LL ENJOY
CLEANER TEETH BY FAR
BURMA-VITA TOOTH
    POWDER

DON'T WASTE POWDER
DOWN THE DRAIN
BY MISSING BRUSH
WITH FAULTY AIM
A DIP DOES IT
BURMA-VITA TOOTH
    POWDER

BETTER TOOTH CLEANSER
LOW EXPENSE
YOUR DRUGGIST
SELLS IT
40 CENTS
BURMA-VITA TOOTH
    POWDER

TOBACCO STAINS
AND STALE BREATH TOO
ARE TWO
OF THE THINGS
IT TAKES FROM YOU
BURMA-VITA TOOTH
    POWDER

1948

ROAD
WAS SLIPPERY
CURVE WAS SHARP
WHITE ROBE, HALO
WINGS AND HARP
BURMA-SHAVE

SPEED
WAS HIGH
WEATHER WAS NOT
TIRES WERE THIN
X MARKS THE SPOT
BURMA-SHAVE

HAT AND TIE
SMART AND CLEAN
SPACE BETWEEN
SPOILED THE SCENE
HE SHOULD USE
BURMA-SHAVE

WHY WORK UP
A DAILY LATHER
ONCE YOU'VE TRIED
WE'RE SURE
YOU'D RATHER
BURMA-SHAVE

THE BOY WHO GETS
HIS GIRL'S APPLAUSE
MUST ACT
NOT LOOK
LIKE SANTA CLAUS
BURMA-SHAVE

IF YOU THINK
SHE LIKES
YOUR BRISTLES
WALK BARE-FOOTED
THROUGH SOME THISTLES
BURMA-SHAVE

WITHIN THIS VALE
OF TOIL
AND SIN
YOUR HEAD GROWS BALD
BUT NOT YOUR CHIN—USE
BURMA-SHAVE

THE MORE
YOU SHAVE
THE BRUSHLESS WAY
THE MORE YOU'LL BE
INCLINED TO SAY—
BURMA-SHAVE

103

SUBSTITUTES AND
IMITATIONS
SEND 'EM TO
YOUR WIFE'S
RELATIONS
BURMA-SHAVE

IT'S NOT
HOW FAST OR SLOW
YOU DRIVE
THE QUESTION IS
HOW YOU ARRIVE
BURMA-SHAVE

HIGHWAYS ARE
NO PLACE
TO SLEEP
STOP YOUR CAR
TO COUNT YOUR SHEEP
BURMA-SHAVE

A MAN WHO PASSES
ON HILLS AND CURVES
IS NOT A MAN
OF IRON NERVES—
HE'S CRAZY!
BURMA-SHAVE

THE MINUTES
SOME FOLKS
SAVE THROUGH SPEED
THEY NEVER EVEN
LIVE TO NEED
BURMA-SHAVE

I'VE READ
THESE SIGNS
SINCE JUST A KID
NOW THAT I SHAVE
I'M GLAD I DID
BURMA-SHAVE

AT SCHOOL ZONES
HEED INSTRUCTIONS!
PROTECT
OUR LITTLE
TAX DEDUCTIONS
BURMA-SHAVE

WE DON'T
KNOW HOW
TO SPLIT AN ATOM
BUT AS TO WHISKERS
LET US AT 'EM
BURMA-SHAVE

REGARDLESS OF
POLITICAL VIEWS
ALL GOOD PARTIES
ALWAYS
CHOOSE
BURMA-SHAVE

PAPER HANGERS
WITH THE HIVES
NOW CAN
SHAVE WITH
CARVING KNIVES
BURMA-SHAVE

THE MIDNIGHT RIDE
OF PAUL
FOR BEER
LED TO A
WARMER HEMISPHERE
BURMA-SHAVE

WILD MEN PULLED
THEIR WHISKERS OUT
THAT'S WHAT MADE
THEM WILD
NO DOUBT—
BURMA-SHAVE

LOOK
DON'T LISTEN
POP IS TRYING
A SUBSTITUTE
INSTEAD OF BUYING
BURMA-SHAVE

A MAN
A MISS
A CAR—A CURVE
HE KISSED THE MISS
AND MISSED THE CURVE
BURMA-SHAVE

LITTLE BO-PEEP
HAS LOST HER JEEP
IT STRUCK
A TRUCK
WHEN SHE WENT TO
   SLEEP
BURMA-SHAVE

WHISKERS
EASY COME,
YOU KNOW
WHY NOT MAKE THEM
EASY GO?
BURMA-SHAVE

(Special Anti-inflation Signs, 1948)

BARGAIN HUNTERS
GATHER 'ROUND
FOR FIFTY CENTS
STILL
HALF A POUND
BURMA-SHAVE
NO PRICE INCREASE

FROM NEW YORK TOWN
TO PUMPKIN HOLLER
STILL
HALF A POUND
FOR HALF A DOLLAR
BURMA-SHAVE
NO PRICE INCREASE

OTHER THINGS HAVE
GONE SKY HIGH
HALF A DOLLAR
STILL WILL BUY
HALF POUND JAR
BURMA-SHAVE
NO PRICE INCREASE

A BIG
IMPROVEMENT
SINCE THE WAR
IS NOW ON SALE
IN YOUR DRUG STORE
BURMA-SHAVE
NO PRICE INCREASE

TUBE IMMENSE
STILL
35 CENTS
EASY SHAVING
LOW EXPENSE
BURMA-SHAVE
NO PRICE INCREASE

LEAP YEAR'S OVER
YOU'RE SAFE, MEN
ALL YOU COWARDS
CAN SHAVE AGAIN
WITH BRUSHLESS
BURMA-SHAVE

JUST THIS ONCE
AND JUST FOR FUN
WE'LL LET YOU
FINISH
WHAT WE'VE BEGUN
? ? ?

HE SAW
THE TRAIN
AND TRIED TO DUCK IT
KICKED FIRST THE GAS
AND THEN THE BUCKET
BURMA-SHAVE

WITH TELEVISION
ON THE SET
STARS ARE
RUNNING OUT
TO GET
BURMA-SHAVE

HEADLINE NEWS
FOR FACE
AND CHIN
NOW IMPROVED
WITH LANOLIN
BURMA-SHAVE

WITH
A SLEEK CHEEK
PRESSED TO HERS
JEEPERS! CREEPERS!
HOW SHE PURRS
BURMA-SHAVE

HIS FACE
WAS LOVED
BY JUST HIS MOTHER
HE BURMA-SHAVED
AND NOW—
OH, BROTHER

MEN
WHO HAVE TO
TRAVEL LIGHT
FIND THE HANDY TUBE
JUST RIGHT
BURMA-SHAVE

WHEN FRISKY
WITH WHISKEY
DON'T DRIVE
'CAUSE IT'S
RISKY
BURMA-SHAVE

SINCE HUBBY
TRIED
THAT SUBSTITUTE
HE'S 1/3 MAN
AND 2/3 BRUTE
BURMA-SHAVE

HIS BEARD
WAS LONG
AND STRONG AND TOUGH
HE LOST HIS
CHICKEN IN THE ROUGH
BURMA-SHAVE

HE ALWAYS USED
A STEAMING TOWEL
AND MUG AND BRUSH
AND LANGUAGE FOUL
'TIL HE TRIED
BURMA-SHAVE

IF YOU
MUST SAMPLE
HER "PUCKER PAINT"
BETTER DRIVE
WHERE TRAFFIC AIN'T
BURMA-SHAVE

SAID ONE WHISKER
TO ANOTHER
CAN'T GET TOUGH
WITH THIS STUFF
BROTHER
BURMA-SHAVE

IT GAVE
SWELL SHAVES BEFORE
NOW YOU'LL LIKE IT
EVEN MORE
THE NEW—IMPROVED
BURMA-SHAVE

OLD DOBBIN
READS THESE SIGNS
EACH DAY
YOU SEE, HE GETS
HIS CORN THAT WAY
BURMA-SHAVE

PULL OFF
THE ROAD
TO CHANGE A FLAT
PROTECT YOUR LIFE—
NO SPARE FOR THAT!
BURMA-SHAVE

TO SOOTHE
AND SMOOTH
YOUR TENDER SKIN
IT'S NOW IMPROVED
WITH LANOLIN
BURMA-SHAVE

ONE BURMA-SHAVE
THE SCHOOL BOY CRIED
AT LEAST
I'LL SMELL
AS IF I TRIED
BURMA-SHAVE

THO TOUGH
AND ROUGH
FROM WIND AND WAVE
YOUR CHEEK
GROWS SLEEK WITH
BURMA-SHAVE

(Minnesota and
Wisconsin, 1949)

IN SEVENTY YEARS
OF BRUSHIN' SOAP ON
GRAMPS COULDA
    PAINTED
THE PENTAGON
USE BRUSHLESS
BURMA-SHAVE

ASHES TO ASHES
FORESTS TO DUST
KEEP MINNESOTA
    GREEN
OR WE'LL
ALL GO BUST
BURMA-SHAVE

THESE THREE
PREVENT MOST
    ACCIDENTS
COURTESY
CAUTION
COMMON SENSE
BURMA-SHAVE

ASHES TO ASHES
FORESTS TO DUST
KEEP WISCONSIN GREEN
OR WE'LL
ALL GO BUST
BURMA-SHAVE

HIS CHEEK
WAS ROUGH
HIS CHICK VAMOOSED
AND NOW SHE WON'T
COME HOME TO ROOST
BURMA-SHAVE

TWINKLE, TWINKLE
ONE-EYED CAR
WE ALL WONDER
WHERE
YOU ARE
BURMA-SHAVE

ON CURVES AHEAD
REMEMBER, SONNY
THAT RABBIT'S FOOT
DIDN'T SAVE
THE BUNNY
BURMA-SHAVE

WHEN
SUPER-SHAVED
REMEMBER, PARD
YOU'LL STILL GET
    SLAPPED
BUT NOT SO HARD
BURMA-SHAVE

HIS BRUSH IS GONE
SO WHAT'LL WE DO
SAID
MIKE ROBE I
TO MIKE ROBE II
BURMA-SHAVE

THE PLACE TO PASS
ON CURVES
YOU KNOW
IS ONLY AT
A BEAUTY SHOW
BURMA-SHAVE

A WHISKERY KISS
FOR THE ONE
YOU ADORE
MAY NOT MAKE HER MAD
BUT HER FACE WILL BE
    SORE
BURMA-SHAVE

BURMA-SHAVE
WAS SUCH A BOOM
THEY PASSED
THE BRIDE
AND KISSED
THE GROOM

THESE SIGNS
WE GLADLY
DEDICATE
TO MEN WHO'VE HAD
NO DATE OF LATE
BURMA-SHAVE

IF YOUR PEACH
KEEPS OUT
OF REACH
BETTER PRACTICE
WHAT WE PREACH
BURMA-SHAVE

A GUY
WHO DRIVES
A CAR WIDE OPEN
IS NOT THINKIN'
HE'S JUST HOPIN'
BURMA-SHAVE

TO KISS
A MUG
THAT'S LIKE A CACTUS
TAKES MORE NERVE
THAN IT DOES PRACTICE
BURMA-SHAVE

THE WHALE
PUT JONAH
DOWN THE HATCH
BUT COUGHED HIM UP
BECAUSE HE SCRATCHED
BURMA-SHAVE

DOESN'T
KISS YOU
LIKE SHE USETER?
PERHAPS SHE'S SEEN
A SMOOTHER ROOSTER! !
BURMA-SHAVE

VIOLETS ARE BLUE
ROSES ARE PINK
ON GRAVES
OF THOSE
WHO DRIVE AND DRINK
BURMA-SHAVE

NO USE
KNOWING
HOW TO PICK 'EM
IF YOUR HALF-SHAVED
WHISKERS STICK 'EM
BURMA-SHAVE

CANDIDATE SAYS
CAMPAIGN
CONFUSING
BABIES KISS ME
SINCE I'VE BEEN USING
BURMA-SHAVE

HE TRIED
TO CROSS
AS FAST TRAIN NEARED
DEATH DIDN'T DRAFT
HIM
HE VOLUNTEERED
BURMA-SHAVE

MY JOB IS
KEEPING FACES CLEAN
AND NOBODY KNOWS
DE STUBBLE
I'VE SEEN
BURMA-SHAVE

HER CHARIOT
RACED 80 PER
THEY HAULED AWAY
WHAT HAD
BEN HUR
BURMA-SHAVE

(Burma-Shave Lotion Jingles, 1950)

SHE WILL
FLOOD YOUR FACE
WITH KISSES
'CAUSE YOU SMELL
SO DARN DELICIOUS
BURMA-SHAVE LOTION

IT HAS A TINGLE
AND A TANG
THAT STARTS
THE DAY OFF
WITH A BANG
BURMA-SHAVE LOTION

USE BURMA-SHAVE
IN TUBE
OR JAR
THEN FOLLOW UP
WITH OUR NEW STAR
BURMA-SHAVE LOTION

BRACING AS
AN OCEAN BREEZE
FOR AFTER SHAVING
IT'S SURE
TO PLEASE
BURMA-SHAVE LOTION

109

FOR EARLY
MORNING
PEP AND BOUNCE
A BRAND NEW PRODUCT
WE ANNOUNCE
BURMA-SHAVE LOTION

THE LADIES
TAKE ONE WHIFF
AND PURR—
IT'S NO WONDER
MEN PREFER
BURMA-SHAVE LOTION

HIS FACE
WAS SMOOTH
AND COOL AS ICE
AND OH! LOUISE!
HE SMELLED SO NICE
BURMA-SHAVE LOTION

1951

(Middle West and East)

I'D HEARD
IT PRAISED
BY DRUG STORE CLERKS
I TRIED THE STUFF
HOT DOG! IT WORKS
BURMA-SHAVE

SOAP
MAY DO
FOR LADS WITH FUZZ
BUT SIR, YOU AIN'T
THE KID YOU WUZ
BURMA-SHAVE

TRAIN WRECKS FEW
REASON CLEAR
FIREMAN
NEVER HUGS
ENGINEER
BURMA-SHAVE

SHE EYED
HIS BEARD
AND SAID NO DICE
THE WEDDING'S OFF—
I'LL *COOK* THE RICE
BURMA-SHAVE

ALTHO INSURED
REMEMBER, KIDDO
THEY DON'T PAY YOU
THEY PAY
YOUR WIDOW
BURMA-SHAVE

TRAIN APPROACHING
WHISTLE SQUEALING
PAUSE!
AVOID THAT
RUNDOWN FEELING!
BURMA-SHAVE

MY CHEEK
SAYS SHE
FEELS SMOOTH AS SATIN
HA! HA! SAYS HE
THAT'S MINE YOU'RE
    PATTIN'
BURMA-SHAVE

UNLESS
YOUR FACE
IS STINGER FREE
YOU'D BETTER LET
YOUR HONEY BE
BURMA-SHAVE

110

ANOTHER
RED SKIN
BIT THE DUST
WHEN PA TRIED
WHAT THESE SIGNS
    DISCUSSED
BURMA-SHAVE

THE BAND
FOR WHICH
THE GRAND STAND
    ROOTS
IS NOT MADE UP
SUBSTI-TOOTS!
BURMA-SHAVE

CAUTIOUS RIDER
TO HER
RECKLESS DEAR
LET'S HAVE LESS BULL
AND LOTS MORE STEER
BURMA-SHAVE

SPRING
HAS SPRUNG
THE GRASS HAS RIZ
WHERE LAST YEAR'S
CARELESS DRIVERS IS
BURMA-SHAVE

BIG BLUE TUBE
IT'S A HONEY
BEST SQUEEZE PLAY
FOR LOVE
OR MONEY
BURMA-SHAVE

PROPER
DISTANCE
TO HIM WAS BUNK
THEY PULLED HIM OUT
OF SOME GUY'S TRUNK
BURMA-SHAVE

SUBSTITUTES
CAN DO
MORE HARM
THAN CITY FELLERS
ON A FARM
BURMA-SHAVE

PAT'S BRISTLES
SCRATCHED
BRIDGET'S NOSE
THAT'S WHEN
HER WILD IRISH ROSE
BURMA-SHAVE

THE HOBO
LETS HIS
WHISKERS SPROUT
IT'S TRAINS—NOT GIRLS
THAT HE TAKES OUT
BURMA-SHAVE

A BEARD
THAT'S ROUGH
AND OVERGROWN
IS BETTER THAN
A CHAPERONE
BURMA-SHAVE

DRINKING DRIVERS
DON'T YOU KNOW
GREAT BANGS
FROM LITTLE
BINGES GROW?
BURMA-SHAVE

I KNOW
HE'S A WOLF
SAID RIDING HOOD
BUT GRANDMA DEAR,
HE SMELLS SO GOOD
BURMA-SHAVE

111

1952

THE WIFE
WHO KEEPS ON
BEING KISSED
ALWAYS HEADS
HER SHOPPING LIST
BURMA-SHAVE

IS HE
LONESOME
OR JUST BLIND—
THIS GUY WHO DRIVES
SO CLOSE BEHIND?
BURMA-SHAVE

PEDRO
WALKED
BACK HOME BY GOLLY
HIS BRISTLY CHIN
WAS HOT-TO-MOLLY
BURMA-SHAVE

MISSIN'
KISSIN'?
PERHAPS YOUR THRUSH
CAN'T GET THRU
THE UNDERBRUSH—TRY
BURMA-SHAVE

CLANCY'S
WHISKERS
TICKLE NANCY
NANCY LOWERED THE
     BOOM
ON CLANCY!
BURMA-SHAVE

A CHIN
WHERE BARBED WIRE
BRISTLES STAND
IS BOUND TO BE
A NO MA'AMS LAND
BURMA-SHAVE

LEAVES
FACE SOFT
AS WOMAN'S TOUCH
YET DOESN'T COST YOU
NEAR AS MUCH
BURMA-SHAVE

WE CAN'T
PROVIDE YOU
WITH A DATE
BUT WE DO SUPPLY
THE BEST DARN BAIT
BURMA-SHAVE

THE WOLF
IS SHAVED
SO NEAT AND TRIM
RED RIDING HOOD
IS CHASING HIM
BURMA-SHAVE

RELIEF
FOR FACES
CHAPPED AND SORE
KEEPS 'EM COMIN'
BACK FOR MORE
BURMA-SHAVE

HIS
TOMATO
WAS THE MUSHY TYPE
UNTIL HIS BEARD
GREW OVER-RIPE
BURMA-SHAVE

HEAVEN'S
LATEST
NEOPHYTE
SIGNALLED LEFT
THEN TURNED RIGHT
BURMA-SHAVE

BETTER TRY
LESS SPEED PER MILE
THAT CAR
MAY HAVE TO
LAST A WHILE
BURMA-SHAVE

HIS ROSE
IS WED
HIS VIOLET BLEW
BUT HIS SUGAR IS SWEET
SINCE HE TOOK THIS CUE
BURMA-SHAVE

TO STEAL
A KISS
HE HAD THE KNACK
BUT LACKED THE CHEEK
TO GET ONE BACK
BURMA-SHAVE

WHY IS IT
WHEN YOU
TRY TO PASS
THE GUY IN FRONT
GOES TWICE AS FAST?
BURMA-SHAVE

WE'VE MADE
GRANDPA
LOOK SO TRIM
THE LOCAL
DRAFT BOARD'S AFTER
   HIM
BURMA-SHAVE

SHE PUT
A BULLET
THRU HIS HAT
BUT HE'S HAD
CLOSER SHAVES THAN
   THAT
BURMA-SHAVE

"NO, NO,"
SHE SAID
TO HER BRISTLY BEAU
"I'D RATHER
EAT THE MISTLETOE"
BURMA-SHAVE

5-STAR
GENERALS
PRIVATES 1ST CLASS
SHOW EQUAL RANK
IN THE LOOKING-GLASS
BURMA-SHAVE

1953

(Middle West and East)

WHEN YOU LAY
THOSE FEW CENTS DOWN
YOU'VE BOUGHT
THE SMOOTHEST
SHAVE IN TOWN
BURMA-SHAVE

GUT RASIERT? ("IF YOU
   WANT A GOOD
   SHAVE?"—GERMAN)
————(CHINESE)
LA MEJOR AFEITADA
   ("THE BEST SHAVE"—
   SPANISH)
THE BEST SHAVE
IN ANY LANGUAGE
BURMA-SHAVE

SUBSTITUTES
ARE LIKE A GIRDLE
THEY FIND SOME JOBS
THEY JUST
CAN'T HURDLE
BURMA-SHAVE

WE'RE WIDELY READ
AND OFTEN QUOTED
BUT IT'S SHAVES
NOT SIGNS
FOR WHICH WE'RE NOTED
BURMA-SHAVE

MEN WHO
HAVE TO
TRAVEL LIGHT
FIND THE 35¢ TUBE
JUST RIGHT
BURMA-SHAVE

IT GAVE
MC DONALD
THAT NEEDED CHARM
HELLO HOLLYWOOD
GOOD-BY FARM
BURMA-SHAVE

A SHAVE
THAT'S REAL
NO CUTS TO HEAL
A SOOTHING
VELVET AFTER-FEEL
BURMA-SHAVE

AROUND
THE CURVE
LICKETY-SPLIT
IT'S A BEAUTIFUL CAR
WASN'T IT?
BURMA-SHAVE

OUR FORTUNE
IS YOUR
SHAVEN FACE
IT'S OUR BEST
ADVERTISING SPACE
BURMA-SHAVE

IF CRUSOE'D
KEPT HIS CHIN
MORE TIDY
HE MIGHT HAVE FOUND
A LADY FRIDAY
BURMA-SHAVE

FEEL YOUR FACE
AS YOU RIDE BY
NOW DON'T
YOU THINK
IT'S TIME TO TRY
BURMA-SHAVE

IF ANYTHING
WILL PLEASE
YOUR JILL
A LITTLE JACK
FOR THIS JAR WILL
BURMA-SHAVE

THAT BAREFOOT
CHAP
WITH CHEEKS OF TAN
WON'T LET 'EM CHAP
WHEN HE'S A MAN
BURMA-SHAVE

IF HARMONY
IS WHAT
YOU CRAVE
THEN GET
A TUBA
BURMA-SHAVE

THE BEARDED DEVIL
IS FORCED
TO DWELL
IN THE ONLY PLACE
WHERE THEY DON'T SELL
BURMA-SHAVE

THIS CREAM
MAKES THE
GARDENER'S DAUGHTER
PLANT HER TU-LIPS
WHERE SHE OUGHTER
BURMA-SHAVE

TOUGHEST
WHISKERS
IN THE TOWN
WE HOLD 'EM UP
YOU MOW 'EM DOWN
BURMA-SHAVE

NO MATTER
THE PRICE
NO MATTER HOW NEW
THE BEST SAFETY DEVICE
IN YOUR CAR IS YOU
BURMA-SHAVE

THESE SIGNS
ARE NOT
FOR LAUGHS ALONE
THE FACE THEY SAVE
MAY BE YOUR OWN
BURMA-SHAVE

HE ASKED
HIS KITTEN
TO PET AND PURR
SHE EYED HIS PUSS
AND SCREAMED "WHAT
    FUR!"
BURMA-SHAVE

THE HERO
WAS BRAVE AND STRONG
AND WILLIN'
SHE FELT HIS CHIN—
THEN WED THE VILLAIN
BURMA-SHAVE

THE SAFEST RULE
NO IFS OR BUTS
JUST DRIVE
LIKE EVERY ONE ELSE
IS NUTS!
BURMA-SHAVE

1955

DINAH DOESN'T
TREAT HIM RIGHT
BUT IF HE'D
SHAVE
DYNA-MITE!
BURMA-SHAVE

THO STIFF
THE BEARD
THAT NATURE GAVE
IT SHAVES
LIKE DOWN WITH
BURMA-SHAVE

TO CHANGE THAT
SHAVING JOB
TO JOY
YOU GOTTA USE
THE REAL MC COY
BURMA-SHAVE

HIS CROP OF
WHISKERS
NEEDED REAPING
THAT'S WHAT KEPT
HIS LENA LEAPING
BURMA-SHAVE

115

THE BLACKENED FOREST
SMOULDERS YET
BECAUSE
HE FLIPPED
A CIGARET
BURMA-SHAVE

THE BIG BLUE TUBE'S
JUST LIKE LOUISE
YOU GET
A THRILL
FROM EVERY SQUEEZE
BURMA-SHAVE

JAR SO BIG
COST SO SMALL
COOLEST
SMOOTHEST
SHAVE OF ALL
BURMA-SHAVE

THE MONKEY TOOK
ONE LOOK AT JIM
AND THREW THE
    PEANUTS
BACK AT HIM
HE NEEDED
BURMA-SHAVE

SLOW DOWN, PA
SAKES ALIVE
MA MISSED SIGNS
FOUR
AND FIVE
BURMA-SHAVE

SUBSTITUTES
CAN LET YOU DOWN
QUICKER
THAN A
STRAPLESS GOWN
BURMA-SHAVE

GRANDPA KNOWS
IT AIN'T TOO LATE
HE'S GONE
TO GIT
SOME WIDDER BAIT
BURMA-SHAVE

FOR SHAVING COMFORT
WITHOUT
A STING
THAT BIG BLUE TUBE
HAS EVERYTHING
BURMA-SHAVE

FREE—FREE
A TRIP
TO MARS
FOR 900
EMPTY JARS
BURMA-SHAVE

6 MILLION HOUSEWIVES
CAN'T BE WRONG
WHO KEEP
THEIR HUSBANDS
RIGHT ALONG IN
BURMA-SHAVE

A CHRISTMAS HUG
A BIRTHDAY KISS
AWAITS
THE WOMAN
WHO GIVES THIS
BURMA-SHAVE

TRY A TUBE
ITS COOLING
POWER
REFRESHES LIKE
AN APRIL SHOWER
BURMA-SHAVE

116

ONE SHAVE LASTS
ALL DAY THROUGH
FACE FEELS
COOL AND
SMOOTHER TOO
BURMA-SHAVE

TAKE
YOUR
TIME
NOT
YOUR LIFE
BURMA-SHAVE

WITHIN THIS VALE
OF TOIL
AND SIN
YOUR HEAD GROWS BALD
BUT NOT YOUR CHIN
BURMA-SHAVE

CATTLE CROSSING
MEANS GO SLOW
THAT OLD BULL
IS SOME
COW'S BEAU
BURMA-SHAVE

DOES YOUR HUSBAND
MISBEHAVE
GRUNT AND GRUMBLE
RANT AND RAVE
SHOOT THE BRUTE SOME
BURMA-SHAVE

1959

THE DRAFTEE
TRIED A TUBE
AND PURRED
WELL WHADDYA KNOW
I'VE BEEN DEFURRED
BURMA-SHAVE

MEN
WITH WHISKERS
'NEATH THEIR NOSES
OUGHTA HAVE TO KISS
LIKE ESKIMOSES
BURMA-SHAVE

THIS COOLING SHAVE
WILL NEVER FAIL
TO STAMP
ITS USER
FIRST CLASS MALE
BURMA-SHAVE

SAID FARMER BROWN
WHO'S BALD
ON TOP
WISH I COULD
ROTATE THE CROP
BURMA-SHAVE

DRINKING DRIVERS—
NOTHING WORSE
THEY PUT
THE QUART
BEFORE THE HEARSE
BURMA-SHAVE

DON'T
TRY PASSING
ON A SLOPE
UNLESS YOU HAVE
A PERISCOPE
BURMA-SHAVE

117

PASSING CARS
WHEN YOU CAN'T SEE
MAY GET YOU
A GLIMPSE
OF ETERNITY
BURMA-SHAVE

USE THIS CREAM
A DAY
OR TWO
THEN DON'T CALL HER—
SHE'LL CALL YOU
BURMA-SHAVE

DON'T LEAVE SAFETY
TO MERE CHANCE
THAT'S WHY
BELTS ARE
SOLD WITH PANTS
BURMA-SHAVE

THE POOREST GUY
IN THE
HUMAN RACE
CAN HAVE A
MILLION DOLLAR FACE
BURMA-SHAVE

AT A QUIZ
PA AIN'T
NO WHIZ
BUT HE KNOWS HOW
TO KEEP MA HIS
BURMA-SHAVE

IF DAISIES
ARE YOUR
FAVORITE FLOWER
KEEP PUSHIN' UP THOSE
MILES-PER-HOUR
BURMA-SHAVE

MANY A FOREST
USED TO STAND
WHERE A
LIGHTED MATCH
GOT OUT OF HAND
BURMA-SHAVE

HE LIT A MATCH
TO CHECK GAS TANK
THAT'S WHY
THEY CALL HIM
SKINLESS FRANK
BURMA-SHAVE

BABY YOUR SKIN
KEEP IT FITTER
OR "BABY"
WILL GET
ANOTHER SITTER
BURMA-SHAVE

THE ONE WHO
DRIVES WHEN
HE'S BEEN DRINKING
DEPENDS ON YOU
TO DO HIS THINKING
BURMA-SHAVE

1960

THIS CREAM
IS LIKE
A PARACHUTE
THERE ISN'T
ANY SUBSTITUTE
BURMA-SHAVE

TEMPTED TO TRY IT?
FOLLOW YOUR HUNCH
BE "TOP BANANA"
NOT ONE
OF THE BUNCH
BURMA-SHAVE

BRISTLES SCRATCHED
HIS COOKIE'S MAP
THAT'S WHAT
MADE POOR
GINGER SNAP
BURMA-SHAVE

DIM YOUR LIGHTS
BEHIND A CAR
LET FOLKS SEE
HOW BRIGHT
YOU ARE
BURMA-SHAVE

WE'VE MADE GRANDPA
LOOK SO YOUTHFUL
HIS PENSION BOARD
THINKS
HE'S UNTRUTHFUL
BURMA-SHAVE

THIRTY DAYS
HATH SEPTEMBER
APRIL
JUNE AND THE
SPEED OFFENDER
BURMA-SHAVE

USE OUR CREAM
AND WE BETCHA
GIRLS WON'T WAIT
THEY'LL COME
AND GETCHA
BURMA-SHAVE

OTHERS CLAIM
THEIR PRODUCT GOOD
BUT OURS
DOES WHAT
YOU THINK IT SHOULD
BURMA-SHAVE

HENRY THE EIGHTH
SURE HAD
TROUBLE
SHORT TERM WIVES
LONG TERM STUBBLE
BURMA-SHAVE

BEN
MET ANNA
MADE A HIT
NEGLECTED BEARD
BEN-ANNA SPLIT
BURMA-SHAVE

ANGELS
WHO GUARD YOU
WHEN YOU DRIVE
USUALLY
RETIRE AT 65
BURMA-SHAVE

DROWSY?
JUST REMEMBER, PARD
THAT MARBLE SLAB
IS DOGGONE
HARD
BURMA-SHAVE

FOREST FIRES
START FROM SCRATCH
SO THINK BEFORE
YOU TOSS
THAT MATCH
BURMA-SHAVE

STATISTICS PROVE
NEAR AND FAR
THAT FOLKS WHO
DRIVE LIKE CRAZY
—ARE!
BURMA-SHAVE

DEAR LOVER BOY,
YOUR PHOTO CAME
BUT YOUR DOGGONE
    BEARD
WON'T FIT
THE FRAME
BURMA-SHAVE

THIS WILL NEVER
COME TO PASS
A BACK-SEAT
DRIVER
OUT OF GAS
BURMA-SHAVE

1963

DON'T LOSE
YOUR HEAD
TO GAIN A MINUTE
YOU NEED YOUR HEAD
YOUR BRAINS ARE IN IT
BURMA-SHAVE

FILM PROTECTS
YOUR NECK
AND CHIN
SO YOUR RAZOR
WON'T DIG IN
BURMA-SHAVE

IF A GIFT
YOU MUST CHOOSE
GIVE HIM ONE
HE'LL LIKE
TO USE
BURMA-SHAVE

A SHAVE
THAT'S REAL
NO CUTS TO HEAL
A SOOTHING
VELVET AFTER-FEEL
BURMA-SHAVE

PEDRO
WALKED
BACK HOME, BY GOLLY
HIS BRISTLY CHIN
WAS HOT-TO-MOLLY
BURMA-SHAVE

IF HUGGING
ON HIGHWAYS
IS YOUR SPORT
TRADE IN YOUR CAR
FOR A DAVENPORT
BURMA-SHAVE

IF OUR ROAD SIGNS
CATCH YOUR EYE
SMILE
BUT DON'T FORGET
TO BUY
BURMA-SHAVE

IN CUPID'S LITTLE
BAG OF TRIX
HERE'S THE ONE
THAT CLIX
WITH CHIX
BURMA-SHAVE

WHEN THE STORK
DELIVERS A BOY
OUR WHOLE
DARN FACTORY
JUMPS FOR JOY
BURMA-SHAVE

A GUY
WHO WANTS
TO MIDDLE-AISLE IT
MUST NEVER SCRATCH
HIS LITTLE VIOLET
BURMA-SHAVE

120

EVERY DAY
WE DO
OUR PART
TO MAKE YOUR FACE
A WORK OF ART
BURMA-SHAVE

IF YOU WANT
A HEARTY SQUEEZE
GET OUR
FEMALE
ANTI-FREEZE
BURMA-SHAVE

THRIFTY JARS FOR
STAY AT HOMES
HANDY TUBES
FOR HIM
WHO ROAMS
BURMA-SHAVE

CAN'T SHAVE DAILY?
TENDER HIDE?
NOW BE HONEST
HAVE YOU
TRIED
BURMA-SHAVE

WE DON'T
KNOW HOW
TO SPLIT AN ATOM
BUT AS TO WHISKERS
LET US AT 'EM
BURMA-SHAVE

THE CHICK
HE WED
LET OUT A WHOOP
FELT HIS CHIN AND
FLEW THE COOP
BURMA-SHAVE

OUR FORTUNE
IS YOUR
SHAVEN FACE
IT'S OUR BEST
ADVERTISING SPACE
BURMA-SHAVE

*   *   *